PHILOSOPHY OF SCIENCE

An Overview
for Cognitive Science

This book belongs to

A. Pierce

Tutorial Essays in Cognitive Science

Advisory Editors

Donald A. Norman
Andrew Ortony

BECHTEL: *Philosophy of Science: An Overview for
Cognitive Science*

BECHTEL: *Philosophy of Mind: An Overview for
Cognitive Science*

GREEN: *Linguistic Pragmatics for
Cognitive Science*

PHILOSOPHY OF SCIENCE

An Overview
for Cognitive Science

WILLIAM BECHTEL
Georgia State University

LEA LAWRENCE ERLBAUM ASSOCIATES, PUBLISHERS
1988   Hillsdale, New Jersey   Hove and London

Lawrence Erlbaum Associates, Inc., Publishers
365 Broadway
Hillsdale, New Jersey 07642

Library of Congress Cataloging in Publication Data
Bechtel, William.
    Philosophy of science: an overview for cognitive science /
William Bechtel.
        p.   cm.
    Bibliography: p.
    Includes index.
    ISBN 0-89859-695-5
    ISBN 0-8058-0221-5 (pbk)
    1. Science—Philosophy. 2. Logical positivism. 3. Cognition.
I. Title.
Q175.B415 1988
153'.01—dc19   87-30463
                                                                CIP

Printed in the United States of America
10 9 8 7 6 5 4 3

This volume is dedicated to the memory of

HANNA

who helped in ways she could not understand

Contents

PREFACE   *xi*

1   THE LOCUS OF PHILOSOPHY
OF SCIENCE   *1*

Introduction: What is Philosophy of
   Science?   *1*
Areas of Philosophy that Bear on Philosophy
   of Science   *3*
Conclusion   *15*

2   LOGICAL POSITIVISM: THE RECEIVED
VIEW IN PHILOSOPHY OF SCIENCE   *17*

Introduction: The Origins of Logical
   Positivism   *17*
The Verifiability Theory of Meaning   *19*
The Deductive–Nomological Model of
   Explanation and the Hypothetico–
   Deductive Model of Theory
   Development   *22*
The Axiomatic Account of Theories   *27*
Summary of Logical Positivism   *29*

3   CHALLENGES TO LOGICAL
POSITIVISM   *32*

Introduction: Challenges to Specific Theses of
Logical Positivism   *32*
The Attack on Confirmation   *32*
Repudiation of the Deductive–Nomological
Model of Explanation   *38*
Critique of the Analytic–Synthetic Dis-
tinction   *41*
A Challenge to the Observation-Theory Dis-
tinction   *44*
Overview of the Criticisms of
Positivism   *48*

4   POST-POSITIVIST PHILOSOPHY OF
SCIENCE   *50*

The Emergence of Historically Grounded
Philosophy of Science   *50*
Kuhn's Challenge: Normal and Revolutionary
Science   *52*
Feyerabend's Attack on Method   *58*
Lakatosian Research Programmes   *60*
Laudan's Research Traditions   *63*
Studies of Scientific Discovery   *65*
Summary of Post-Positivist Philosophy of
Science   *68*

5   THEORY REDUCTION AS A MODEL FOR
RELATING DISCIPLINES   *71*

Introduction: Relating Disciplines by Relating
Theories   *71*
The Theory Reduction Model and the Unity
of Science Program   *72*
Arguments Against Trying to Reduce Psy-
chology to Neuroscience   *76*

Reduction as Facilitating the Co-Evolution of
   Psychology and Neuroscience   *82*
The Elimination of Folk Psychology in Favor
   of One that is Reducibile   *87*
Implications of the Theory Reduction Model
   for Relating Psychology and Neuroscience   *92*

6   AN ALTERNATIVE MODEL FOR
        INTEGRATING DISCIPLINES   *94*

   Introduction: The Desire for an Alternative
      Model   *94*
   Shortcomings of the Theory Reduction
      Model   *94*
   Darden and Maull's Conception of Interfield
      Theories   *97*
   Interfield Theories Between Cognitive Science
      and Neuroscience   *101*
   Interfield Theories Within Cognitive
      Science   *110*
   Conclusions Concerning Cross-Disciplinary
      Research   *117*

POSTSCRIPT   *119*

REFERENCES   *120*

AUTHOR INDEX   *130*

SUBJECT INDEX   *134*

Preface

As one of the several contributing disciplines to cognitive science, philosophy offers two sorts of contributions. On the one hand, *philosophy of science* provides a metatheoretical perspective on the endeavors of any scientific enterprise, analyzing such things as the goals of scientific investigation and the strategies employed in reaching those goals. Philosophy of science thus offers a perspective from which we can examine and potentially evaluate the endeavors of cognitive science. On the other hand, *philosophy of mind* offers substantive theses about the nature of mind and of mental activity. Although these theses typically have not resulted from empirical investigation, they often have subsequently figured in actual empirical investigations in cognitive science, or its predecessors. Because the two roles philosophy plays in cognitive science are quite different, they are introduced in separate volumes. This one focuses on philosophy of science, whereas issues in philosophy of mind are explored in *Philosophy of Mind: An Overview for Cognitive Science.*

The strategy for this volume is to present a variety of views from philosophy of science that have figured in discussions about cognitive science. Some of these views are no longer widely accepted by philosophers of science. Nonetheless, they have been and, in some cases, remain influential outside of philosophy. Moreover, some older views have provided the starting point for current philosophical thinking that is done against a backdrop of previous endeavors, with a recognition of both their success and failure.

After an introductory chapter that introduces some of the other domains of philosophy that are pertinent to philosophy of science, this book falls into two main parts. Chapters 2, 3, and 4 explore general views about the nature of science and scientific explanation. Chapter 2 focuses on Logical Positivism, a comprehensive view of the character of scientific theories and their status as claims to knowledge that was developed in the first half of this century. As I discuss in chapter 3, many of the doctrines of Logical Positivism have been criticized and the position is no longer widely accepted. But it continues to have wide influence in science. Its influence is particularly noticeable in the standard accounts of scientific method presented in the early chapters of introductory science texts. One reason Logical Postivism remains influential is that there has been no successor perspective that has gained comparable acceptance. A new perspective, however, is arising amongst those philosophers who have taken seriously the importance of actual scientific practice, particularly as revealed through the history of science. This new approach, which began with Thomas Kuhn's *The Structure of Scientific Revolutions*, (1962/1970), is discussed in chapter 4.

Chapters 5 and 6 explore an issue in philosophy of science that is particularly pertinent to practitioners of cognitive science. This is the question of the proper way of relating inquiries in different disciplines of science. A legacy of Logical Positivism, the Theory Reduction Model offers one widely discussed model for relating disciplines. It focuses on the relationship between the cognitive sciences and neuroscience and advocates the view that cognitive science theories should be reducible to neuroscience theories. This model, which has recently been defended in the influential text of Patricia Churchland, *Neurophilosophy* (1986), is discussed in chapter 5. A number of philosophers, however, have come to reject the Theory Reduction Model and have sought alternative views of the relationships between disciplines. One of these is discussed in chapter 6. It provides not only a different perspective on the relationship of cognitive science to neuroscience but also on the interactions of disciplines within cognitive science itself.

For those not previously acquainted with philosophy, some comments about how to approach philosophical material are in order. Although it used to be widely proclaimed that philosophical claims do not require empirical evidence, this view is much less accepted today. It remains the case, however, that philosophical claims tend to be fairly far removed from empirical evidence. Therefore, there tends to be much greater room for argument as to the virtues of particular claims than in many cases where empirical evidence is readily at hand. In considering the views discussed in this book, the reader should bear in mind the controversial and argumentative character of philosophical inquiry. This means that rather than simply accepting or rejecting a view, the reader should consider the possible kinds of arguments that might be made on behalf of or against the views presented. The reader, thereby, enters into the argument itself, and does not remain a passive obervser. Although the accumulated efforts of philosophers provide a resource for anyone taking up these issues, the issues are not the exclusive prerogative of philosophers; scientists are encouraged to engage with the issues themselves and to reach their own conclusions.

ACKNOWLEDGMENTS

I have received help and support from a number of institutions and persons in developing this text. First, thanks to Larry Erlbaum for inviting me to write this text. Although it was not as easy a project as it seemed it might be when he invited me, I have learned much from it. Special thanks are also due to Andrew Ortony for his valuable editorial advice and comments. Jim Frame was my research assistant through much of the writing of this text and provided invaluable assistance, particularly in organizing and coordinating bibliographical materials. Robert McCauley provided detailed and most useful comments on several versions of this chapter. Adele Abrahamsen, Robert Almeder, Patricia Churchland, Donald Norman, Robert Richardson, and William Wimsatt also read all or part of various versions of this text and offered substantial comments, for which I am most grateful. Finally, a Georgia State University Research Grant provided essential support for developing the text, and is gratefully acknowledged.

1

The Locus of Philosophy of Science

INTRODUCTION: WHAT IS PHILOSOPHY OF SCIENCE?

This volume is devoted to introducing some of the basic issues in philosophy of science to the practitioners of the various disciplines of cognitive science: cognitive psychology, artificial intelligence, cognitive neuroscience, theoretical linguistics, and cognitive anthropology. Philosophy of science is a field devoted to analyzing the character of scientific investigations. It attempts to answer such questions as: What is a scientific explanation? To what extent can scientific claims ever be justified or shown to be false? How do scientific theories change over time? What relations hold between old and new theories? What relations hold, or should hold, between theoretical claims developed in different fields of scientific investigation? A variety of answers that philosophers have offered to these and other questions are examined in subsequent chapters of this book. Before turning to the concrete views philosophers have offered, however, it is useful to put the attempts to address these questions in perspective.

Since antiquity, philosophers have been interested in science for the reason that science seems to represent the most rigorous attempt by humans to acquire knowledge. This has led a number of philosophers to seek a criterion by which they could distinguish scientific endeavors and the resulting knowledge claims from other knowledge claims humans have advanced (e.g., ones based on mysticism, intuition). Philosophers, however, have not been the only people who have been fascinated by science and who have attempted to explain how it works. Historians have long been interested in the development of science, partly as an area of intellectual history. More recently, social historians and sociologists have focused on science and the social context in which scientific investigation occurs. There have even been a few investigations by psychologists directed at the scientific endeavor itself. Although there have often been bitter controversies between philosophers, historians, sociologists, and psychologists of science as to which discipline's methodology provides the best tool to explicate the nature of science, there is beginning to emerge a cluster of practitioners from a variety of disciplines who take science as their subject matter. Increasingly, the term *science of science* is being used to characterize these investigations.

As the term *science of science* suggests, the inquiry into the nature of science, whether carried out by philosophers or others, is a reflexive endeavor, using the very skills that are employed in human inquiry to understand the human race's most systematic example of inquiry—science. This reflexive inquiry, especially as done by philosophers, has had profound consequences on science itself. Many scientists have been seriously concerned with the issues of philosophy of science. Such concern is particularly likely to be expressed in the context of open debates within the scientific community when questions arise as to proper scientific strategy or legitimate style of scientific explanation. (The recent history of psychology has witnessed such controversies in the battles between behaviorism and cognitivism, whereas cognitive science generally is currently witnessing such a battle between connectionists and those advocating rules and representations accounts of mind.) Some scientists who become concerned about philosophy of science issues may become contributors to the literature in philosophy of science (e.g., Polanyi, 1958). Most scientists, however, simply adopt a philosophy of science that is popular, or that suits their purposes, and cite it as authority. This proclivity to borrow positions from philosophy is rather common but poses serious dangers because what may be quite controversial in philosophy may be accepted by a particular scientist or group of scientists without recognizing its controversial character.[1] One of the objectives of this volume is to attempt to alleviate this situation in cognitive science by providing a brief, introductory account of the various competing philosophical perspectives on the nature of science. Then, if readers adopt a particular view of what science is, they will do so with some awareness of the alternatives and of some of the controversies that surround the position.

There are no sharp boundaries that divide the analyses of science advanced by philosophers from those offered by historians, sociologists, or psycholo-

---

[1] The fact that scientists have invoked a variety of positions developed in the philosophy of science literature requires that in this text I do not simply introduce the most prominent current positions, but also those that have been influential in the recent past and that still live on in the thinking of many scientists.

gists. In general, however, philosophers have tended to be more interested than practitioners of these other disciplines in the reasoning processes actually or ideally employed by scientists and have sought to identify criteria that give scientific claims their objective validity. Moreover, philosophers bring to their analyses of science a background that involved training in other areas of philosophy. As a result, they often call upon the conceptual tools developed in other areas of philosophy in analyzing science.[2] To provide nonprofessional philosophers the necessary background to understand and appreciate the claims made by philosophers of science, the remainder of this chapter is devoted to providing a brief introduction to other areas of philosophy that bear upon philosophy of science.

AREAS OF PHILOSOPHY THAT BEAR
ON PHILOSOPHY OF SCIENCE

Philosophy as practiced in the modern Western world is probably best characterized as an attempt to develop systematic and defensible answers to such questions as: What are proper modes of reasoning? What are the fundamental categories of things? How can humans know about the natural world? How should humans behave? These questions define the basic domains of philosophy—logic, metaphysics, epistemology, and value theory. All of these bear to some degree on philosophy of science. The following is a brief account of the basic issues in each of these domains and of how these issues impact on philosophy of science.

Logic

The central issue in logic is the evaluation of argument. An argument is simply a set of statements, some of which serve as premises or support for others, that are called *conclusions*. Two criteria are relevant to evaluating arguments: Is the argument of such a sort that if the premises were true, the conclusion would also have to be true? and Are the premises true? An argument that satisfies the first of these criteria is traditionally called *valid* whereas an argument that satisfies both is called *sound*. The discipline of logic is primarily concerned with the first of these criteria, that is, with determining whether the argument is of a sort where the truth of the premises guarantees the truth of the conclusion. The truth preserving ability of an argument turns out not to depend on the content of what is stated in the argument but only on the

---

[2] A useful introduction to philosophical methodology is Woodhouse, 1984.

form of the argument. The concept of argument form can be explicated intuitively as that which remains when all the words or phrases bearing content have been replaced by variables, provided that the same substitution is made for all instances of words or phrases that have the same content. (For example the logical form of the sentence "It is raining and it is cold" might be "x and y," where x and y are variables.)

There have been two basic accounts of logical form in the history of philosophy. One goes back to Aristotle and gives rise to what is called *syllogistic logic*. The second was developed in the later 19th and early 20th centuries, principally through the work of Frege and Russell, and constitutes what is commonly referred to as *symbolic logic*. Syllogistic logic can be construed as a logic of classes, and uses information about what class an object belongs to or information about class inclusion to determine other relationships. The basic form of reasoning employed is the syllogism in which two statements about membership relations between objects and classes of objects are used to support an additional statement. The following is a typical valid syllogism:

> All humans are mortal.
> All Greeks are human.
> _____
> Therefore, all Greeks are mortal.

Although syllogistic logic proved useful for capturing a variety of valid forms for arguments, there were a significant number of arguments that could not be captured. Modern symbolic logic was developed in order to overcome this shortcoming. There are two components of symbolic logic. The first is commonly spoken of as *sentential logic* or *propositional logic*, and the second is called *quantificational logic* or *predicate calculus*. Sentential logic takes simple complete sentences or propositions such as "it is raining" as units. It then uses truth functional connectives to build more complex, compound sentences. A connective is truth functional if the truth or falsity (truth value) of the compound sentence can be ascertained just by knowing the connective employed and the truth value of the component sentences. Although the connectives of sentential logic are defined in terms of precise rules that deviate from those governing the corresponding English words, the main connectives are generally expressed using the words "not," "and," "or," "if ———, then . . . ," and "if and only if." Through a device known as a truth table, one can show how the truth values of various compound sentences depend on those of the component sentences (represented by the letters A and B). The truth value of a sentence is indicated by placing a T or F in the appropriate place in the table. The truth tables for sentences formed using the basic connectives just listed are shown here (a common symbol for the connective is indicated below the English statement for the compound):

English gloss	not A	A and B	A or B	If A, then B	A if and only if B
Notation 1:	$-A$	$A \cdot B$	$A \lor B$	$A \rightarrow B$	$A \leftrightarrow B$
Notation 2:	$\overline{A}$	$A \cap B$	$A \cup B$	$A \supset B$	$A \equiv B$

A	B					
T	T	F	T	T	T	T
T	F	F	F	T	F	F
F	T	T	F	T	T	F
F	F	T	F	F	T	T

The truth table for most of these connectives is just what one would expect. The troublesome one is the "if A, then B" connective, which is somewhat counterintuitively assigned the truth value true whenever A (the antecedent) is false. Part of the motivation for this interpretation can be captured by considering under what circumstances the statement could be recognized as false. The only such circumstance is where A is true and B (the consequent) is false. One important point to notice, though, is that given this interpretation of the "if ———, then . . . " connective, it is not proper to think of it as equivalent to implication. Logicians, rather, speak of it as the "material conditional."[3]

Derivations in sentential logic use premises and conclusions consisting of either simple statements or compound statements constructed from simple statements using these truth functional connectives. There are many such forms of valid derivations. One of the most important of these, known as *modus ponens* or "affirming the antecedent," is the following:

> If A, then B.
> A
> _____
> Therefore, B.

---

[3] There is a connection between the material conditional and implication. If a conditional statement is a tautology, that is, a statement that cannot be false, then one can speak of the consequent as implied by the antecedent. But in ordinary conditional sentences, this does not hold. This treatment of the "if__, then . . ." connective results in a number of theorems that some logicians have found paradoxical and so labeled the *paradoxes of material implication*. One theorem is the statement " $- A \rightarrow (A \rightarrow B)$", which says that if A is false, then if A then B is true. If "if__, then . . . "is read as "__ implies . . . ", then one gets the paradoxical sounding statement "not A implies that A implies B". Another example of a paradox of material implication is the theorem "$(A \cdot - A) \rightarrow B$". Reading this using implies yields "the contradiction A and not A imposes any statement whatsoever." Logicians have differed as to whether there is anything really paradoxical here and whether any change is needed to remedy the situation. Those who defend the material conditional simply insist that it ought not to be read as "implies." (For a criticism of the material conditional based on the paradoxes, see Anderson & Belnap, 1975, and for a defense of the material conditional, see Hughes & Cresswell, 1968.)

Another very important form, known as *modus tollens* or "denying the consequent," has the following form:

> If A, then B.
> Not B.
> _____
> Therefore, not A.

Treating these and some other basic forms as rules that license inferences from statements of the form of the two premises to statements of the form of the conclusion yields a system of *natural deduction*. In such a system you begin with a set of premises and apply a series of such rules to derive an ultimate conclusion.

Of course, not all forms of argument are valid. There are, in fact, two invalid forms that closely resemble the valid forms above. The first, known as *affirming the consequent*, has the following form:

> If A, then B.
> B
> _____
> Therefore, A.

The second, known as *denying the antecedent*, has the form:

> If A, then B.
> Not A
> _____
> Therefore, not B.

The forms can be recognized as invalid by substituting "it rains" for A and "the game will be cancelled" for B. Now assume in each case that the premises are true and consider whether the conclusion might be false. Because it clearly could be false, the argument form is not valid.

Quantificational logic expands on the power of sentential logic by exposing the inner structure of the basic statements used in sentential logic and showing how a variety of valid forms rely on this structure. The structure in question is the basic subject–predicate structure, as is found in the sentence "the sky is blue." To represent this structure, replace the subject terms (those referring to objects) with lower-case letters from the beginning of the alphabet and predicate terms with upper-case letters from the middle of the alphabet. Thus, the earlier sentence may be represented as "Pa," where P = "is blue" and a = "the sky." The predicate term in this case covers only one object, and so is termed *monadic*. It is also possible to have relational predicates that take two or more objects. For example, "taller than" is a relational predicate and the sentence "Carol is taller than Sarah" may be represented Tab.

In addition to representing statements referring to specific objects, quantificational logic allows for generalizations that assert either that a statement is true for any object or for at least one. Thus, the statement "All dogs have hearts" can be symbolized as $(x)(Fx \rightarrow Gx)$, Which is read "For all x, if x, is a dog, then x has a heart." Similarly, the statement "There exists a white dog" is symbolized as $(\exists x)(Fx \cdot Gx)$, which is read "There exists an x such that x is white and x is a dog. In natural deduction systems for quantificational logic there are specific rules governing when it is permissible to introduce or remove these quantifiers. These rules give quantificational logic a power deductive structure. (For an introduction to symbolic logic and many issues concerning logic relevant to cognitive science, see McCawley, 1981.)

The interest in logic, however, goes beyond the ability to use it to produce detailed proofs. There are interesting properties that can be proven of logical systems themselves. Many of these proofs of what are called *metatheorems* were developed as part of an endeavor to use logic to provide a foundation to arithmetic. Frege, for example, set out to show that all the truths of mathematics could be rendered in terms of arithmetic and that all the principles of arithmetic could be rendered in terms of logic. (This project is known as the reduction of mathematics to arithmetic, and arithmetic to logic.) Frege had to abort his program when Russell pointed out a contradiction in the system Frege had developed. Logic requires consistent systems because if a system is inconsistent it is a trivial exercise to derive any statement from it. One of the basic things that must be established for any logical system, therefore, is that it is consistent. The demonstration that Frege's system for deriving arithmetic from logic was inconsistent undercut the interest in that system.

The program of reducing arithmetic to logic turned out to be impossible, but pursuit of this program resulted in number of important findings. For example, in addition to consistency another important property of a logical system is completeness. A complete system is one in which the axiom structure is sufficient to allow derivation of all true statements within the particular domain. Kurt Gödel established that quantificational logic is complete—any statement that must be true whenever the premises are true can, in principle, be derived using the standard inference rules for quantificational logic. But the fact that a system is complete does not mean that a procedure exists to generate a proof of any given logical consequence of the premises. If such a procedure exists the system is decidable. Sentential logic is decidable, and so are some restricted versions of quantificational logic. But Church proved that general quantificational logic is not decidable. In general quantificational logic, the mere fact that we have failed to derive a result from the postulates does not mean that it could not be derived; it may be that we simply have not yet constructed the right proof. Of even more significance to the program of grounding mathematics in logic was Gödel's proof that, unlike quantificational logic, there is no consistent axiomatization of arithmetic that is complete. This is referred to as the *incompleteness of arithmetic* and is commonly presented as the claim that for any axiomatization of arithmetic there will be a true statement that cannot be proven within the system. (For detailed treatments of these theorems, see Quine, 1972, and Mates, 1972.)

Some of these theorems about logic have played important roles in the development of computer science. Other claims of logic, which are commonly accepted as true but which are not or cannot be proven, have figured prominently in motivating the use of computers to study cognition. An example is Church's thesis, which holds that any decidable process is effectively decidable or computable, which is to say that it can be automated. If this thesis is true, then it follows that it is possible to implement a formal system on a computer that will generate the proof of any particular theorem that follows from the postulates. The assumption that this thesis is true has buttressed the use of computers in studies of cognitive processes. Assuming that cognition relies on decidable procedures, this thesis tells us that these procedures can be implemented on a digital computer as well as in the brain. (For a challenge to this assumption, see Smolensky, in press.) Symbolic logic has played a more general role in artificial intelligence. Many have assumed that the procedures of symbolic logic characterize much of human reasoning, and because these procedures can readily be implemented on a computer, many investigators have tried to develop simulations of human reasoning using computers equipped with these inference procedures. For our purposes here, however, the interest in logic is that numerous philosophers have tried to explicate scientific theories as logical structures and the structure of scientific explanations in terms of formal logical derivations. We see this prominently in chapters 2 and 5.

Metaphysics

Metaphysics seeks to determine what are the basic or fundamental kinds of things that exist and to specify the nature of these entities. Historically, interest in metaphysics centered on such issues as whether a supreme being or a creator god exists, whether there are mental phenomena or spiritual phenomena that are different from physical phenomena, or whether there is such a thing as free will (for sample writings, see Taylor, 1978). In more recent times it has addressed the question of the kinds of entities that we can include in scientific theories. For example, are mental events the kinds of things that should be posited in a theory of human action? The set of entities posited is generally said to specify the ontology to which the theory is committed.

It is important to note that the character of metaphysical questions is generally taken to be different than the character of ordinary empirical questions such as whether there are any living dinosaurs. With such empirical questions we rely on such techniques as ordinary observation to settle the issue. Ontological questions are thought to be more fundamental and not resolvable by ordinary empirical investigations. It was thought that to address the classical questions of the existence of God or of minds separate from bodies required a kind of inquiry that went beyond ordinary empirical investigation. Sometimes it was claimed that such issues could be addressed simply through the tools of logic. For example, the ontological argument for God's existence tried to argue from the idea of God as a perfect being to the actual existence of God. It claimed this could be done by invoking the principle that if God did not exist, there would a more perfect being—a being just like God but who actually existed. Thus, the assumption that God does not exist is claimed to be contradictory, so God must exist. The modern ontological questions concern how we should set up the categories through which we conduct our empirical inquiry. The question of the appropriate categories arises prior to empirical observation and so cannot be easily settled by means of such observation.

To many nonphilosophers both classical and contemporary questions of ontology seem peculiarly remote and unproductive. Of what value would it be to have an answer to an ontological question? The very character of ontological questions suggests that they lack practical significance. If ontological differences do not entail physical differences, it would seem that one could hold whatever ontology one wanted and still deal with the physical world in much the same way. When the challenge is put in this way, philosophers often find themselves hard put to provide a satisfactory answer. A number of philosophers, in fact, have tried to divert attention away from metaphysical issues. The logical positivists, whom I discuss in the next chapter, claimed that most classical questions of ontology were meaningless, whereas Ludwig Wittgenstein (1953) tried to convince readers that when philosophers raised such issues they were letting their language go on a holiday, not raising real questions at all.

Other philosophers have sought to reduce the distance between ontological inquiries and empirical ones. Quine (1953/1961b; 1969a), for example, proposed that when we settle on a scientific theory we thereby settle the question of what ontological scheme we accept. Invoking the framework of quantificational logic, where all the terms referring to objects can be represented as variables in quantified expressions, Quine offers the maxim "to be is to be the value of a bound variable" (1953/1961b, p.15; i.e., the objects to which we attribute properties in our theories are the ones whose existence we accept). Although this attempt to place ontological questions in the context of scientific inquiry may seem particularly attractive when we consider how perplexing the issues are otherwise, we should not think that thereby we really avoid them. What this proposal overlooks is that many of the debates over the adequacy of scientific theories have focused on the ontology assumed by the theory. This has been particularly true in recent psychology, where there have been active disputes over whether to count mental events as causal factors in an explanatory theory. But such questions are not peculiar to psychology. In physics and biology as well, disputes between theories have often turned on ontological issues as much as on empirical issues. For example, there was a long controversy between Cartesians and Newtonians during the 17th and 18th centuries over the legitimacy of appeals to action at a distance (as is countenanced by the Newtonian concept of gravity). Embryology at the end of the last century was torn by a prolonged battle between vitalists and mechanists over the appropriate kind of explanation for developmental phenomena.

Citing these historical examples may engender the response that although at the time the ontological issues loomed large, these issues have now been resolved and what resolved them was the success of a scientific theory. There is something correct about this observation. These controversies do show that empirical considerations are relevant to settling ontological questions. But they do not show that the ontological questions are insignificant to the development of science and can simply be ignored. An examination of contemporary physics and biology shows that in these disciplines ontological issues are still central. In quantum physics, theorists are split over whether a unified account of the basic forces of nature is needed, or whether a dualistic account is acceptable. In evolutionary biology there is active disagreement over whether selection works only on individuals or whether it also works on higher level entities like groups or species (see papers in Sober, 1984, for an introduction to this debate). Similar controversies exist in cognitive science even amongst those who accept the legitimacy of mentalistic explanation. Barwise and Perry (1983), for example, proposed an approach to semantics according to which the semantic content is not totally represented in symbols within the cognitive system but depends on the context in which the cognitive system is embedded. They maintained, moreover, that the legitimacy of inference also depended on the context and could not be specified totally in formal principles governing the manipulation of symbols. In this they seem to have violated an ontological principle, the formality constraint, which Fodor (1980) has articulated for cognitive science. According to the formality principle, all information that is to affect the system's behavior must be formally represented. Thus, the question is raised as to whether the formality condition is a proper ontological principle for cognitive science. (For a sample of this debate, see Fodor, 1987, and Barwise, 1987.)

The evaluation of theories often depends on judging the coherence of their ontological assumptions. Theories that make inconsistent ontological assumptions, or ones that contemporary researchers find unacceptable, are criticized in much the same way as theories that make false empirical predictions. Yet, in some way empirical criteria must be applicable if ontological issues are to be settled. The link between ontological issues and empirical inquiry stems from the fact that although ontological issues often play a role in developing a particular kind of research program, the ability of such a research program to produce a progressive tradition of theorizing often affects subsequent judgments about the adequacy of the ontological position underlying the program.

The previous paragraph may suggest the false view that because ontological issues are partly settled by the adequacy of the research programs based on them, we need to wait for the verdict of history on the fruitfulness of such research programs to evaluate ontological positions. However, the dialogue is often much more interactive than this. From the collective experience of attempting to develop accounts of nature, we can evaluate whether particular ontological positions are likely to be satisfactory, or will lead to unsolvable problems. When we recognize that certain assumptions are likely to produce problems, we can anticipate them. Sometimes these very problems can be avoided by reshaping the theory within a different ontological framework. Then, in order to avoid the problems, it is useful to take seriously the ontological commitments being made and to reformulate hypotheses in a framework that will avoid the problems.

Metaphysical questions are clearly important to science, but, as I have noted, some philosophers of science, including the Logical Positivists, have tried to dispense with them as pseudo-issues. Nonetheless, other philosophers, whom I consider in chapter 4, have argued for a prominent role for metaphysical questions in determining the direction and progress of science. Further, even the Logical Positivists, in their model of theory reduction, provided a framework for unifying the ontologies of different theories, as we see in chapter 5. Thus, metaphysical issues are quite pertinent to philosophical accounts of science.

Epistemology

Whereas metaphysics is concerned with delimiting the fundamental categories of what exists, epistemology is concerned with the question of what knowledge is and how it is possible. Epistemological discussion often has been prompted by skeptical doubts that what we believe might be false. Although there have been skeptics throughout history who have challenged people's knowledge claims, perhaps the most profound skeptical challenge is found in the 17th century philosopher Descartes (1641/1970), who began his *Meditations on First Philosophy* by directing as much doubt as possible toward our ordinary beliefs. He started with some common strategies for raising doubts. For example, he pointed out that we are all aware of having been deceived by our senses at some point (e.g., by perceptual illusions) and questioned how we can know at any particular time that we are not being similarly deceived.

Further, he noted how we have sometimes had dreams that seemed so lifelike that we thought we were awake and that even afterwards we could not distinguish from real experience. Finally, he proposed a hypothesis that, if true, would call nearly every belief we have into question. This hypothesis posits that we are the creation of an evil genius whose major preoccupation is to make us believe falsehoods. To accomplish this, the evil genius arranges for it to appear as if we lived in the physical world and had a physical body and knew other people, but this is all a grand illusion created as part of its attempt to deceive us. Once such doubts are raised, the task for epistemology is to overcome them and show that we do have real knowledge.

The general assumption that stems from the ancient Greek philosopher Plato is that knowledge is related to belief but has a special status. One feature of knowledge that differentiates it from belief is that what is known must be true, whereas what is believed may be false. At a minimum, therefore, knowledge seems to involve true beliefs. But this is not sufficient because we would not credit someone whose true belief was a lucky guess with knowledge. So commonly, knowledge is taken to be *justified true belief*. This raises the question as to what constitutes justification. Before we consider that question, however, we need to note that several epistemologists have challenged the definition of knowledge as justified true belief. They have proposed a variety of counterexamples that satisfy the definition but do not seem to constitute knowledge. A typical countererexample involves a case where a belief is true and where the person has information that seems to justify it, but where the relationship between the justifying information and the object of belief is inappropriate. For example, a person might correctly believe that there was an object 10 feet ahead where the justification was provided by perception. However, the scene might have been so arranged with mirrors so that, although there actually was an object 10 feet in front of the person, the object seen is an identical object that is behind the person. As a result, the person would not really know that the object was there (see Gettier, 1963). Defenders of the definition of *knowledge* as justified true belief have attempted to refine the definition of *knowledge* to handle such examples, resulting in a continuing sequence of counterexamples and redefinitions.

After defining *knowledge*, the central question for epistemologists has been to specify what kind of justification is required for knowledge. Within the history of epistemology several approaches have been pursued (e.g, Plato and Descartes both argued for some form of *a priori* justification for knowledge), but most contemporary epistemologists adopt one of two basic approaches to justification—foundationalism or coherentism. The foundationalist approach compares knowledge with an architectural structure. The support for most knowledge claims are a set of foundational claims, with other pieces of knowledge being derived from these. The challenge confronting the foundationalist is to identify the foundational claims. Generally, foundationalists appeal to perceptual beliefs. One approach, now generally not in favor, proposed that there were direct objects of perception, called *sense-data*, that consisted of simple perceptual qualities, like patches of color. The view held that we directly perceive and so have completely justified beliefs about these sense-data, and that all other knowledge is logically derived from them. This approach has been abandoned, partly because philosophers came to question the idea that we had direct awareness of sense-data and partly because the prospects of ever deriving knowledge of worldly objects from such primitive foundations began to appear impossible. Contemporary foundationalists generally appeal to a criterion such as being indubitable or self-warranted to identify foundational beliefs (see Chisholm, 1976, 1982). A recent variant on this approach has been to seek a foundation in a reliable belief making process (see Goldman, 1986).

The coherentist approach rejects the whole idea of exernal foundations and instead appeals to the relationship between beliefs to find justification. The idea is that a set of beliefs either cohere with each other or are inconsistent with each other. Some of those that cohere provide justification to each other such that, even if no one of these beliefs can be supported independently from the rest, the whole network stands together (see Lehrer, 1974). The coherentist generally faces two challenges. One is to explicate what kind of relationship between a set of beliefs is required to make the whole set warranted. We can imagine simple sets of statements, all of which might be false but which cohere well with one another. The coherentist needs to establish criteria to specify which of such sets of coherent beliefs are to count as justified and hence as knowledge. The second challenge is to show why anyone should take the coherence of a set of beliefs, however that coherence is characterized, as providing knowledge. (For an introductory set of readings in contemporary epistemology that introduces both foundationalism and coherentism, see Chisholm & Schwartz, 1973.)

Generally, the weakness of the foundationalist approach coincides with the strength of the coherentist approach and vice versa. The foundationalist tries to identify some beliefs that take us outside of our belief structure and put us in direct contact with the external world, but faces the difficulty of identifying which beliefs can stand on their own as knowledge claims. Most of our beliefs, even our perceptual beliefs, seem to be interlinked and to depend on each other. The coherentist obviates this need by always focusing on the interconnection of beliefs. However, the coherentist then faces the problem of explaining why coherence should provide us any indication of how nature is. At the current time, sophisticated versions of both approaches can be found in the epistemological literature and each side has tried to coopt some of the strengths of the other. In epistemological debates, however, one essentially witnesses a conflict between inconsistent intuitions as to what is critical in making a belief into knowledge.

Issues of epistemology are obviously of great relevance to philosophy of science, especially insofar as scientific claims are taken as a paradigmatic claims to knowledge. The tradition of Logical Positivism, discussed in the following chapter, adopts the foundationalist approach and tries to justify our knowledge of scientific theories by showing how such theories are grounded in perception. Critics of the Positivist program, as we in chapters 3 and 4, have attacked the idea of an objective observational base to ground scientific theories, thereby raising fundamental questions as to how scientific beliefs are to be justified.

Before leaving this topic, I should note that some notable philosophers such as Quine (1969b, 1973) have concluded that the classical endeavors in epistemology are fundamentally misguided. Often, this challenge takes the form of denying that we can ever answer the skeptic who asks us to justify our knowledge in a way that is immune from further doubt. One way to abandon classical epistemology is to reject the claim that what is known must be true and focus instead on justified beliefs. This, however, raises objections from those who find a logical inconsistency in saying "Smith knew that it was raining, but was wrong." The other way to abandon classical epistemology is to dismiss the concept of *knowledge* as useless and focus only on the question of what justifies *belief*. Generally, those who make this move also tend to adopt a quite different attitude toward justification. Rather than looking for kinds of justification that guarantee truth, they look for modes of justification that increase the likelihood of reaching true judgments, or at least judgments that one will continue to affirm as true in the future. Within this context, empirical information about how human beings process information and make judgments become relevant. Various parts of cognitive science, including cognitive psychology and artificial intelligence, as well as historical accounts of how humans have performed on reasoning tasks, can provide pertinent information. Hence, such an approach to epistemology is commonly spoken of as *naturalized epistemology*. One particular approach that has received a good deal of discussion in recent years involves comparing the belief acquisition process to the process of evolution, with the idea that more adequate beliefs are comparable to well-adapted species and that the mode of acquiring adequate beliefs involves a winnowing process much like natural selection. (See Campbell, 1974a, Popper, 1972, Toulmin, 1972, Hooker, 1987 for positive treatments of this idea; Thagard, 1980, for a critical response; and Bradie, 1986, for an evaluative overview.)

Value Theory

Several of the areas of philosophy that I have surveyed already have a normative dimension. The term *normative* implies concern with standards that *ought* to be adhered to, not simply describing how things are. Logic, for example, is generally viewed as normative in that it seeks the standards for good arguments, although epistemology is normative in that it aspires to standards for evaluating whether someone has knowledge or only belief. Many of the other domains of philosophy, however, are even more clearly concerned with values or with analyzing the source of values. These include ethics, which attempts to identify norms that should guide human behavior; political philosophy, which analyzes how one might determine what kind of state should be created; and aesthetics, which analyzes what should count as works of art. I am clustering all of these areas together under the label *value theory*. One of the central issues common to all areas of the value theory is the question of whether one can rationally adjudicate questions of value and establish norms. Hume argued that one cannot logically derive a normative claim, a claim about what should be, from a descriptive claim, a claim that something is the case. This suggests that normative statements cannot be rationally defended. A central task pursued by many philosophers interested in value theory has been to try to show that Hume (1740/1888) was wrong and that we can derive normative statements from purely descriptive information, or at least rationally defend our value statements. Others who have acquiesced and accepted Hume's judgment have tried to show what status should be accorded to value statements if one does not try to rationally justify them.

For the most part, questions of value theory are quite removed from the concerns of philosophy of science. There are, however, some points of intersection that should be briefly noted. A number of scientists, especially in more theoretical and mathematical disciplines of science, often speak of the elegance of a particular theory, suggesting that theoretical accounts of nature ought to adhere to an aesthetic standard. One version of this perspective is the view that a simpler account of nature is to be preferred to a more complex one if they are empirically equally adequate. The interaction between moral and political theory and philosophy of science has also developed in recent decades, especially as it becomes more clearly recognized that knowledge can have consequences. Thus, there have been a variety of arguments that some issues, such as genetic bases of intelligence, should not be scientifically investigated because of the potential harm that might come from knowing the answers to such questions. In this regard, some have argued that scientific investigation needs to be construed as a form of human action and subject to the same moral criteria as any other human action. The result is that philosophy of science will need to include discussion of moral issues that might arise from scientific research. This is not, however, a matter that is further pursued in this text.

CONCLUSION

Philosophy of science is focused on such questions as: What constitutes a scientific explanation? and How are scientific knowledge claims to be justified? As such, philosophy of science draws upon other areas of philosophy, especially logic, metaphysics, and epistemology. In subsequent chapters I examine a number of influential views of science advanced by philosophers and note some of their strengths as well as raising a variety of objections. As was noted at the outset, this inquiry has consequences because scientists often use perspectives from philosophy of science either to support their own work or criticize that of their opponents. As we proceed to look at a variety of answers in subsequent chapters, it is important to bear in mind that these issues are controversial and that there are a variety of different views on most important questions in philosophy of science. The answers philosophers have offered to these questions are fallible and philosophers should not be used as final authorities to resolve important questions in science. Rather, their views ought to be carefully examined and evaluated by all scientists who invoke them in making decisions about their scientific endeavors.

Before proceeding, however, a final qualification is needed. Twentieth century philosophy in Western countries has been broadly split into two traditions. What is commonly called *analytical philosophy* has been the dominant tradition in most of the English speaking world as well as much of Scandinavia and parts of Germany. A prominent focus of the analytic movement has been the logical analysis of language and statements, including scientific statements, made in language. *Existentialism* and *phenomenology*, on the other hand, have dominated philosophical work on much of the European continent. These traditions have been much more concerned than the analytic tradition with the subjective elements of human existence and have attempted to describe these systematically and explore their implications for a variety of human endeavors, including scientific inquiry. This is not the proper place for a detailed discussion of the relative merits of the two approaches. Both have shown considerable interest in science, but from adopted quite different perspectives toward science. The views discussed in this text are primarily drawn from the analytic tradition. However, the approach to philosophy of science pursued by this tradition has been so transformed in recent decades that it no longer bears clear affinities to its philosophical heritage of logical analysis but is more concerned with giving a faithful account of actual scientific practice.

2

Logical Positivism:
The Received View in
Philosophy of Science

INTRODUCTION: THE ORIGINS
OF LOGICAL POSITIVISM

Logical Positivism emerged and became the dominant philosophical perspective on science in the first half of the century. Although its popularity has declined in recent decades, it continues both to set the agenda for many ongoing philosophical discussions and to provide the criteria that many scientists, including those in the cognitive sciences, use to judge what is good science. Logical Positivism arose in Austria (the Vienna Circle), Germany (the Berlin School), and Poland in the 1920s, but many of its principal theorists, including Rudolf Carnap, Herbert Feigl, Hans Reichenbach, and Carl Hempel moved to the United States with the rise of Nazism. Their views have subsequently been treated as part of the mainstream of "analytic philosophy" as practiced in the English-speaking world. Many of these founders were physicists and mathematicians who recognized that developments in physics, particularly the emergence of quantum mechanics and relativity theory, seemed incompatible with accepted wisdom about the nature of scientific investigations. As admirers of science generally, and especially of the new physics, the Logical Positivists set out to explicate the nature of science with a view to showing what made it a reliable source of knowledge.

The two terms that comprise the name "Logical Positivism" provide a good introduction to it. The term *positivism* comes from the philosophy of August Comte, an early 19th century philosopher who was skeptical of philosophical systems and of metaphysics generally and emphasized knowledge based on experience. He took science to be the paradigm of knowledge, citing as its strength the fact that it was empirically grounded in experience. More influential than Comte in providing this part of the foundation for Logical Positivism, however, were the classical 17th century Empiricists, especially David Hume, and their more contemporary descendants such as Ernst Mach. In accord with both Comte and the empiricists, the Logical Positivists maintained that all knowledge must be grounded on experience,[1] although the specific nature of this grounding was a matter of some dispute.

The term *logical* reflects the role that modern symbolic logic (see chapter 1) played in the views of the Logical Positivists. The Positivists used the resources of logic in attempting to provide a formal rendering of the structure of science. Because ordinary discourse often fails to adhere to the standards of symbolic logic, the Positivists found it necessary to propose the use of formal languages designed to adhere to the canons of symbolic logic in order to present their analyses. Their hope was that such a clear, formal presentation of science would ground the claim that science is a source of knowledge as well as help to resolve issues in science that had resulted from lack of precision.

An obvious difficulty that any practicing scientist will recognize in this program is that actual scientific thinking often fails to adhere to the strict canons of logical thinking. However, the Logical Positivists were not attempting to account for all scientific activity. First, they distinguished between *the context of discovery*, in which scientific hypotheses were developed, and *the context of justification*, in which they were rationally assessed (see Reichenbach, 1966). They held that the context of discovery might well be nonlogical. To cite a famous example, Kekule is supposed to have developed his proposal for the structure of the benzene radical while gazing upon the pattern of a flame from a burning log. He interpreted the flames as atoms dancing in snakelike arrays, and when one of the snakes seemed to grasp its tail, forming a ring structure, that suggested to him the ring structure for benzene. On the other hand, the process by which the correctness of this idea is tested is thought to depend on the logical relation between the hypothesis and the evidence that supports it. Hence, the Positivists proposed to leave to psychologists the task of explaining how scientists discovered new ideas and focused their attention on articulating the procedures of justification, whereby scientific theories could be shown to be true on the basis of evidence.

Even in the context of justification, however, the Positivists recognized that practicing scientists often do not adhere to the canons of formal logic. What the Logical Positivists maintained was that justificatory reasoning of scientists, if it was good, could be "reconstructed" to accord with the con-

---

[1] To capture this aspect of their position, some of the logical positivists subsequently came to prefer the label "Logical Empiricism" for their endeavor.

strual of scientific reasoning based on modern logic. The Positivists were, in effect, proposing normative standards for science. They were claiming that science that adhered to these standards, or that could be reconstructed so as to conform to them, constituted good science that provided knowledge about the world.

In order to clarify the basic conception of scientific justification advanced by the Logical Positivists, I explore three critical features of their account. The first is the theory they advanced about how terms in scientific laws had meanings (which captures the Positivists' allegiance to empiricism). The second is the deductive-nomological method of explanation and the related hypothetico-deductive model of justification, and the last is the axiomatic view of theories. (These last two together reflect the commitment to logical analysis.) Because the Positivists devised their conception of science with the physical sciences principally in mind, I rely heavily on examples from those disciplines in initially presenting the Positivists' program, and consider how Positivism might apply to examples from cognitive science in the concluding section of this chapter.

THE VERIFIABILITY THEORY
OF MEANING

The Logical Positivists attributed many of the confusions and uncertainties of science, particularly those found in the social and behavioral sciences, to unclarity in the language. Even more strongly, they claimed that the quandaries that beset other areas of human inquiry, including politics, religion, and areas of philosophy like metaphysics, resulted from unclear use of language. When language is not governed by strict rules of meaning, the Positivists contended, confusion sets in and people may end up producing utterly meaningless statements. In calling a statement meaningless, the Positivists were not merely asserting that the statement was false but something worse—the statement was not really understandable. The kind of statement the Positivists had in mind is a statement like "God is love." Consequently, they viewed theological debates, for example, not as substantive debates for which there were objective answers, but simply as confused discourse. The remedy for such confusion was to attend carefully to the principles governing meaningful discourse and to restrict oneself to those domains where language could be used meaningfully. The Positivists did admit that language could serve other functions than making true or false statements. For example, they thought that literature and poetry could be used to arouse emotional responses or inspire action. But science, they maintained, was concerned with truth and therefore had to restrict itself to discourse for which clear principles of meaningfulness were available.

In their discussions of meaning the Positivists followed the classical Empiricists in linking knowledge to experience, but they advocated one important change. The classical Empiricists treated ideas as the units of thinking and viewed these ideas as causal products of sensory experience. The Logical Positivists rejected ideas as fuzzy entities. Rather, they took linguistic entities—sentences and words—to be the basic vehicles of meaning. They proposed the criterion of verification to explain how these linguistic entities could be appropriately related to experience. According to this criterion, *the meaning of a sentence was the set of conditions that would show that the sentence was true*. Although these conditions would not actually occur if the sentence was false, we could still state what would be the case if it was true. Because only sentences and not individual words could be true or false, the meaning of words had to be analyzed in terms of their roles in sentences. This account of meaning became known as the *verifiabilty theory of meaning*.

Some sentences, the Logical Positivists maintained, could be directly verified through experience. Sensory exposure could tell us directly that these sentences were true or false. The Positivists referred to these sentences variously as *protocol sentences* or *observation sentences*. There was considerable disagreement amongst Positivists as to which sentences counted as such. Some, like the early Carnap (1928/1967), restricted observation sentences to those characterizing our phenomenal experience (e.g., "I am sensing a blue color patch now"). Others, like Nuerath (1932), maintained that sentences about observable parts of the world (e.g., "The sun is shining") could be directly verified. For the most part, Positivists took observation sentences to refer to physical states of the world, producing a bias toward that which is physically observable.

Other sentences in a language could not be verified directly through experience. This is particularly true of sentences that contain theoretical terms (e.g., *force*) that do not directly refer to observable features or objects. To explicate the meaning of these terms the Positivists focused on ways in which the truth or falsity of sentences using these terms could be determined indirectly via other sentences that were observational. Here logical analysis became important, for the Positivists had to explain the logical relationship between two sentences whereby one could serve to explicate the meaning of the other. Initially, a number of Positivists proposed to "translate" all sentences referring to theoretical entities into observation sentences (Carnap, 1923). Because they limited themselves to the tools of symbolic logic, the kind of translation with which the Positivists were concerned was not aimed at preserving the connotation of the theoretical sentence, but at identifying sentences that were true under the same empirical conditions. Thus, translations consist of biconditional sentences that assert that one statement (the theoretical statement) is true if and only if another, possibly complex statement (the observation statement) is true. These statements have an unusual characteristic. Because they only articulate the meaning of one sentence in terms of another sentence, they do not depend on experience in any way and so cannot be refuted by experience. Such statements are often referred to as *analytic statements* to distinguish them from ordinary sentences whose truth depends upon how the world is.[2]

This attempt to explicate the meaning of all scientific discourse in terms of observation conditions is closely related to the very influential doctrine, associated with the American physicist and mathematician Percy Bridgman (1927), of operational definitions. According to this doctrine, in introducing a theoretical concept, it is necessary to specify operations through which one can confirm or disconfirm statements using that term. Bridgman's notion of an operational definition extends the Positivists' conception of an observation term by supplying procedures for producing the requisite observations.

One of the issues in cognitive science to which the verifiability theory of meaning has been applied is the question of whether machines can think. In order to render this into a meaningful question, the Positivists required that it be translated into a sentence that can be confirmed or disconfirmed observationally. Turing's (1950) famous test for machine thinking provides the kind of operational definition of thinking that would be required. Turing proposed that we should accept a machine as thinking when we could not distinguish its behavior (e.g., in answering questions and carrying on a dialogue) from that of a thinking human being. Of course, we also confront problems in deciding whether another human being is thinking, or is simply an automaton. The verificationist theory of meaning, however, advocates the same treatment of this case—explicate what thinking is in terms of the kinds of behavior a thinking being would perform. This treatment construes the concept of thought as referring not to some unobservable activity but as something detectable in the behavior of organisms or computers. (For a philosophical analysis of thought in terms of behavior, see Ryle, 1949.)

The criterion that theoretical terms have to be translatable into observational terms was quickly recognized to be too strong. First of all, it is common for theoretical terms to be linked with experience in more than one way. This is particularly true for measurement terms for which there may be several different observational criteria. Generally, scientists will not accept just one of these as the definition, but view them as giving alternative criteria. Some of these may be discounted if several of the others all support a common measurement. This practice cannot be understood if one insists that there be a single definition translating theoretical terms into observational terms. Secondly, a number of theoretical terms, for example, dispositional terms like *soluble*, may not be translatable into observational terms. An object's property of being soluble cannot be correlated directly with observable features

---

[2] The latter kind of sentence is then referred to as a *synthetic statement*.

of the object except when the object is placed in water. Many soluble objects will never be placed in water. Even worse, the dispositional term cannot be translated into a conditional sentence (e.g., if it is placed in water, then it will dissolve). The reason is that in symbolic logic a sentence of the form "if———, then . . ." is defined as true if the antecedent is false (see previous chapter). This would make any object that was never placed in water soluble.

To account for the meaning of such terms, which contemporary science seems clearly to require, positivists attempted to weaken their verifiability conditions. Carnap (1936, 1937) proposed that a dispositional term like *soluble* could be translated by the following sentence (which he termed *reduction sentence*):

> "If x is placed in water, then x will dissolve if and only if x is soluble."

Such a reduction sentence overcomes the previous objection because it does not imply that something never placed in water is soluble. It also has the consequence that under conditions where the test conditions are never investigated (e.g., where the object is destroyed before it can be placed in water) we will not be able to determine the truth of the theoretical sentence. Unfortunately, this means that the initial aspirations of the verifiability criterion are not achieved because there will be reduction sentences for terms even though we may be powerless to verify the actual applicability of the term in specific instances. But at least, according to the Positivists, we know what conditions we claim hold when we make a statement using the term.

THE DEDUCTIVE–NOMOLOGICAL MODEL OF EXPLANATION AND THE HYPOTHETICO-DEDUCTIVE MODEL OF THEORY DEVELOPMENT

So far we have focused on the criterion for assessing the meaningfulness of scientific statements, but the goal of science is not only to make meaningful statements, or even true meaningful statements. For the Logical Positivist, the basic tasks of science were to explain phenomena in nature and to predict their occurrence. These tasks, as we see, were closely intertwined. Following a tradition that goes back at least to Aristotle, the Positivists maintained that explaining an event consisted of deriving a statement describing that event from statements of scientific laws and statements describing antecedently known empirical facts (initial conditions). Thus, deduction plays a central role in their account of explanation and the Positivists adopted what has been termed the "covering law" or "deductive–nomological" (D–N) model of scientific explanation. This basic model is represented by the following schema, in which L_1 through L_n represent general laws, C_1 through C_n represent initial conditions, and E represents the event to be explained:

$$L_1, L_2, \ldots L_n$$
$$C_1, C_2, \ldots C_n$$
_____
$$\text{Therefore, } E$$

The laws that are required for this schema are conditional statements of the form "If X happens, Y will happen." The initial conditions tell us that X has happened. An example of a law statement would be a statement of the form "If a human being is deprived of vitamin C for a certain number of days, the individual will suffer scurvy." The initial condition might then be that a particular individual had been deprived of vitamin C for that number of days. This would provide an explanation of why the individual experienced scurvy. (For an extended discussion, see Hempel, 1965, and Nagel, 1961.)

A couple of features of this general schema of explanation should be noted. First, in order to explain an event, according to the Logical Positivists, it was not sufficient simply to point to a factor that might have caused the event. For example, noting that someone threw a rock at it would not be sufficient to explain why the window broke. An explanation requires a complete derivation of the event from general laws and known facts. Hence, laws play a central role in any explanation. Second, according to this view there is a symmetry between explanation and prediction. They both have the same logical structure such that a derivation of the sort required for explanation would, if carried out before the event, serve to predict the event. The difference is simply a temporal matter that predictions are made before the event has occurred, while explanations are offered for events that have already taken place. Some critics have found this symmetry to be counterintuitive, because sometimes, at least, it seems that we may be in position to explain events that we could not have predicted. For example, after the fact, we may explain traffic accidents even though we never acquire sufficient information about the initial conditions or develop a precisely articulated law that would predict accurately when accidents would occur. We may be able to assign responsibility for an accident to a faulty traffic light, but still not have enough information about the movement of vehicles to predict when an accident would occur. (This type of objection is developed further by Scriven, 1962, whom I discuss further in the next chapter.) The Positivists, however, defend this symmetry, and would reject the claim that we have explained the event if we do not have sufficient information to determine just what accident would occur. If we do develop such information, then we can both explain why the particular accident occurred, and, if we had had the information in advance, we would have been able to predict it.

So far we have focused on deterministic explanations, where every time the initial conditions satisfy the law statements, the consequent will follow. Several positivists attempted to generalize this model to include probabilistic laws that hold that given a specified set of conditions, there is a certain probability that an effect of the specified kind will follow. In such a case we do not have a strict deduction of a statement specifying the event that occurred, but something weaker—a demonstration that a certain kind of event was likely. For example, taking a particular drug may cure a disease most of the time, but not in all cases. In such a case we can explain and predict the cure by appealing to the statistical relationship and the fact that the person had the disease and took the drug. Hempel (1962) thus proposed a modification of the D–N model to allow for "inductive–statistical" explanations where one could infer that the event was highly probably. This strategy only worked, however, for events whose probability was raised above .5 by the statistical regularity and the initial conditions. Events that follow upon one another with relatively low frequency, such as acquiring lung cancer after smoking, could neither be explained nor predicted on this account. Many critics found this consequence of the attempt to broaden the D–N approach to cover statistical explanation counterintuitive (see chapter 3).

Returning to the context of deterministic laws, we should note that a deduction of the kind called for by the D–N model of explanation would only count as an explanation if the laws adduced in the explanation were true. The law statements required in D–N explanations are generalizations that cover a potentially unlimited number of events. That is, they are statements of the form "If any object contains exposed iron, then it is subject to rusting" $[(x)(Fx \rightarrow Gx)]$. The fact that such statements apply to a potentially infinite number of states of affairs may, at first, seem to render them unverifiable and thus, given the verification theory of meaning, meaningless. But the Positivists took the very deductive relationships used in D–N explanations to give meaning to the law statements. Moreover, they viewed the events that were explained by the laws as themselves providing the evidence for the truth of the law. Thus, the previous law statement would be confirmed by particular events of iron rusting.

The Positivists called the procedure for developing scientific laws the *hypothetico–deductive* (H–D) method. The basic idea of the H–D method is that scientists begin with an event that requires explanation. Hempel (1966), cites the example of Semmelweis' work during the 1840s on childbed fever to illustrate the method. Semmelweis noted that a large proportion of the women who delivered children in his hospital contracted an often fatal illness known as "puerperal fever" or "childbed fever." The rate, moreover, was much higher in the wards where physicians handled the deliveries than in wards where midwives were in charge. To explain that it was necessary to propose a hypothesis from which the difference between the two wards could be derived. Prior to Semmelweis, a number of hypotheses had been proposed, but none seemed adequate to explain the differences between the two wards. Semmelweis, however, found a clue when a fellow physician came down with a fatal disease much like childbed fever after receiving a puncture wound while performing an autopsy. Semmelweis offered the hypothesis that "cadaveric matter" picked up during the autopsy might be the agent responsible both for his colleague's disease and the cases of childbed fever.

Having developed a hypothesis (recall that for the Positivists how hypotheses were arrived at was not a matter for logical inquiry), the task was to discover whether the hypothesis was true. If it was, it could provide the law needed to explain the event. Semmelweis would be reasoning circularly if the only evidence he offered for the hypothesis was the event he started out with. But the hypothesis is a general statement and so could be tested by considering other initial conditions, and deriving predictions about what would happen under those conditions. If these predictions turn out to be true, the initial hypothesis would be confirmed; if the predictions turn out false, the hypothesis would be disconfirmed. In Semmelweis' case, he proposed a test in which physicians would begin to wash their hands in chlorinated lime before examining patients. He predicted that the rate of childbed fever in the physicians' ward would decease (this was a consequence derived from the new initial conditions and the hypothesized law). This prediction proved true, providing evidence for the truth of the hypothesis.

Both the deductive–nomological model of explanation and the hypothetico–deductive model for developing explanations seem eminently plausible when one considers cases like that of childbed fever. Both, however, encounter some basic difficulties that were recognized by the Positivists themselves. The D–N model requires that one of the premises in the deductive explanation of an event be a law. Explicating what makes a statement into a law, however, is a difficult problem given the tools of symbolic logic upon which the Positivists relied. It was clear that a law statement had to be a true general statement of the form: "For all x, if x is F, then x is G" $[(x)(Fx \rightarrow Gx)]$. (For example, for any person, if the person is infected with cadaveric matter, then the person contracts childbed fever.) However, it was also clear that this is insufficient because we would not want to count all true general statements as laws. For example, if it were true that I only carried $1 bills in my wallet, then the following would be a true general statement: for all x, if x is a bill in my wallet, then it is a $1 bill. But this intuitively is not a law (Goodman, 1947). The reason is that there does not seem to be any reason except chance or my perversity for me to carry only $1 bills in my wallet. It is commonly thought that laws are more than general statements that happen to be true. We think they tell us something about the limits of how things *must be*.

Sometimes people try to characterize what is distinctive about laws by saying that they must be able to support counterfactual claims, that is, claims about what would be the case if the facts were different than they are. Counterfactual claims commonly take the form "If something were F (infected with cadaveric matter), then it *would be* G (ill with childbed fever)." This rules out the previous example concerning currency in my pocket because few of us think that if someone put a $10 bill in my wallet, it would become a $1 bill. The problem, however, is that counterfactual claims cannot be represented within basic symbolic logic. Some philosophers have proposed a variety of logics to handle counterfactual claims that are commonly referred to as *modal logics*. Such logics contain operators that specify what is possible or what is necessary. (See Stalnaker, 1968, for an attempt to apply modal logics to scientific laws.) Some Positivists (e.g., Carnap, 1956; Reichenbach, 1956) explored this avenue. However, for strict Positivists, the commitment to the verifiability account of meaning prevented use of modal logics. Nothing in experience could ground a distinction between common generalizations and modal statements because the only evidence we can acquire is that which supports the generalization. Counterfactual circumstances, by definition, do not arise and hence cannot be called upon to mark the difference between a true generalization and a true counterfactual. The only route open to the Positivists, therefore, was to attempt to differentiate law statements from merely true generalizations in terms of how the statements are accounted for by theories. Generalizations that are supported by theories have greater empirical support and hence are more likely to be true in new circumstances (Hempel, 1966). The role of such theories in the Positivists' view of science is the focus of the next section. What is important to note here is that being explained by a theory is the only factor to which the Positivist can appeal to distinguish laws from universal generalizations.

The use of symbolic logic also poses problems for the hypothetico–deductive analysis of hypothesis development. It was recognized by David Hume (1740/1888) that inductive evidence could never establish definitively the truth of any general claim. It is always possible that there might a counterevidence to a general claim that simply had not been discovered as yet. Yet the Positivists wanted to maintain that collecting evidence confirming a hypothesis should increase our confidence in its truth. The reason is clear: Confirmed predictions were the only vehicle recognized by the H–D model for gathering evidence for the truth of hypotheses or laws. But given the commitment to standard symbolic logic, even this is in jeopardy. A number of paradoxes were brought forward to challenge the assumption that confirming evidence should strengthen our belief in particular hypotheses.

One of these paradoxes (commonly known as the *Raven Paradox*) depends on the fact that a law statement of the form

For all x, if x is F, then x is G

is logically equivalent to the statement

For all x, if x is not G, then x is not F.

If F stands for *raven* and G for *black*, then the law "All ravens are black" (e.g., for all x, if x is a raven, then it is black) is logically equivalent to "All things that are not black are not ravens" (e.g., For all x, if x is not black, then it is not a raven). To test the first statement, the H–D model would lead us to examine ravens to see if they are black. The more black ravens we encounter, the greater support for the law (as long as we do not encounter ravens that are not black). But the form to which it is logically equivalent only requires us to examine things that are not black and test the prediction that these things will not be ravens. Every nonblack object that you see that is not a raven will confirm the putative law. So you can sit in the room you are now in and test the law that all ravens are black by making sure all the nonblack objects in the room are not ravens. Something clearly seems to have gone wrong!

Confronted by this and other logical peculiarities,[3] the Positivists sought to refine their account of how evidence could confirm hypotheses (see Swinburne, 1971, for a review). The Positivists' commitment to symbolic logic and, in particular, their commitment to laws being fundamentally universal generalizations, however, lay at the heart of these problems. Hence, they were not easily resolved. Moreover, the moves made to rescue Positivism tend to cloud the clear and intuitive picture of the nature of explanation and confirmation that the Positivists' account seemed to offer.

THE AXIOMATIC ACCOUNT OF THEORIES

I noted previously that the Positivists proposed to differentiate laws from accidental generalizations by appeal to the fact that laws can be grounded in scientific theories. When they spoke of theories, the Positivists generally had in mind such large-scale frameworks as Ptolemy's or Copernicus' astronomy, which offered basic accounts of how various celestial bodies moved with respect to each other; Newton's mechanical theory, which offered a basic set of principles relating the motion and attraction of objects; and the germ theory of disease, which offered an account of what caused diseases and how they spread. The idea underlying the Positivist account of theories is that just as they claimed that an event is explained by showing how a statement

---

[3] Another such paradox was Goodman's (1955) "grue" paradox. By definition, an object is grue if it is green before time t and blue after that time. If time t is the year 2050 and we are looking at an object before that year and it appears green, we cannot conclude that the object is green. It might actually be grue. Give the possibility of predicates like "grue" it is impossible to determine what hypothesis is actually confirmed by current evidence.

about the event could be derived from a law, so a law (e.g., a law about the free fall of bodies on the surface of the earth) is explained by deriving it from a theory (e.g., Newton's mechanical theory that specified the force of attraction between any two objects). A theory was thus a structured network of statements from which one could derive specific laws (see Hempel, 1966, and Nagel, 1961). A model of the kind of structure they had in mind is found in Euclidean geometry. At the core of Euclidean geometry are a set of primitive terms and postulates. From these postulates, various axioms can be derived. In a like manner, the Positivists proposed that scientific theories could themselves be rendered as deductive structures in which we could identify a set of primitive terms and postulates. The particular laws would be the axioms that we could derive from these assumptions and postulates.

Thus, for the Positivists, a theory is best viewed an axiomatic structure.[4] Although the Positivists recognized that most theories are not presented in such an axiomatic fashion, they claimed that theories could be axiomatized and offered thermodynamics as an example of a theory which had already been axiomatized. They argued, moreover, that such axiomatization could be helpful to scientists. First, it would introduce rigor into scientific discourse, forcing scientists to be precise in characterizing notions that might otherwise be left intuitive and hence unclarified. Second, it would allow scientists to discover some of the consequences of a theory that they had not anticipated. This would allow them to make additional predictions so as to carry out additional tests of the theory and to appreciate the full explanatory power of the theory.

The Logical Positivists also envisioned that the process of axiomatizing theories could bring unity to science. Imagine, for example, that the Copernican theory of astronomy has been successfully axiomatized. Someone might question the basic postulates of astronomical theory and demand an explanation of them. How should a Copernican respond? The Positivists proposed that the Copernican should proceed just as in other cases where an explanation is sought—by seeking more general statements from which the Copernican laws could be derived. In this case, the more general statements would not be statements about astronomical phenomena, because the assumption is that the astronomical theory was already complete. Rather, the Copernican would try to generalize beyond astronomy, developing general physical principles that apply not just to astronomy but to all other physical objects. This is the enterprise Newton carried out successfully, showing that the basic postulates of astronomical theory are themselves axioms derived from a more

---

[4] The Positivists and their descendants have not been in total agreement on the virtues of axiomatization. Suppes (1968), Kyburg (1968), and Feigl (1970) have been strong advocates of axiomatizing theories, while Hempel (1970) points to the limits of such an approach. Generally, axiomatization has been most favored by those focusing on examples from physics, but some philosophers of biology (notably, Williams, 1970, and Rosenberg, 1985) have been strong advocates of solving problems by first axiomatizing the theories in question.

basic physical theory. Astronomy was thus subsumed within physics. Eventually, the Positivists proposed, all sciences could be subsumed into one theoretical edifice, that of unified science.

The process of unifying science by deriving the principles of one science from those of another is commonly spoken of as *theory reduction*. I return to this topic in chapter 5. For now, however, we should note just a few aspects of this view. First of all, it assumes that science is basically a cumulative enterprise. Scientists continually incorporate the results of previous inquiries into ever larger theoretical networks. Second, it views the laws of specialized disciplines, such as physiology or psychology, as derivative laws which, in principle, can be derived from the most basic laws of physics. Hence physiology and psychology, according to this view, will eventually be subsumed within physics as a special application of physical laws. The compartmentalization of science into separate disciplines with their own theories and laws is, for the Positivists, simply a result of the incompleteness of current inquiry. Once we have axiomatized the theories in these disciplines, we will be able to integrate them into one broad account of nature.

SUMMARY OF LOGICAL POSITIVISM

The Logical Positivists offered a systematic and highly attractive view of the project of science. They proposed a theory of meaning that showed how scientific discourse was grounded in sensory experience and thus certain to be meaningful. They provided an account of explanation that used deduction to show how particular events could be explained by laws and an account of confirmation that showed how particular events provided evidence for the laws that were developed. Finally, they showed how the laws of each science could be unified in to axiomatic structures and ultimately grounded in a unified account of nature. Many have found this view of science very attractive. (For further details regarding the Positivists' program, see Suppe, 1977, and Brown, 1979. For a useful collection of readings from many of the Positivists, see Ayer, 1963.)

In concluding this chapter it is worth briefly indicating how these doctrines of Logical Positivism might apply to cognitive science. A number of psychologists of an earlier generation adopted the Positivists' conception as a guide for developing their own science. A variety of the doctrines discussed here had significant impact on a number of behaviorists such as Spence and Skinner. This is particularly true of the verificationist theory of meaning, which was taken by many behaviorists to show the illegitimacy of positing or recognizing mental events except insofar as they could be explicitly linked to observable behaviors. The deductive–nomological model of explanation and the axiomatic view of theories also had profound influence on such behaviorists as Clark Hull, whose learning theory was a highly developed axiomatic structure. Moreover the hypothetico–deductive method of theory development has been emphasized in the teaching of scientific methodology in psychology throughout the reign of both behaviorism and cognitivism.

Although Positivism has been less popular during the recent reign of cognitivism, one can illustrate the basic claims of the Positivists equally by showing how they could be applied to theories of recent cognitive science. A central field of research over the past decade has been the structure of human concepts and the processes of categorization. Philosophers and others have commonly thought of categories as mathematical sets, that is, structures with well-defined conditions of membership (generally referred to as *necessary* and *sufficient conditions* of membership). This idea was already challenged by the philosopher Wittgenstein (1953), who used the example of the concept "game," and questioned what could be the necessary and sufficient conditions for being a game. He argued that there were no necessary and sufficient conditions that defined the category games, but that games were only related by "family resemblance." To develop a scientific theory of concepts, the Positivists would insist, it is necessary first to provide criteria for the meanings of terms used in the theorizing, especially terms like *concept*. Eleanor Rosch (1975, 1978) developed a tool that might be viewed from a Positivist's perspective (although probably not from Rosch's) as providing an operational definition of concepts. She asked subjects to evaluate the typicality of particular instances of category. From this she showed that with a variety of categories, both natural and artificial, subjects would not only quite willingly evaluate how typical a particular example of the category was but also that there would generally be a high rate of intersubject agreement (but see Barsalou & Sewall, 1984). Thus, most Americans would judge a robin to be a very typical bird, and a chicken to be quite atypical. From the Positivists' perspective, the typicality measure can be construed as providing a basis in observation in terms of which we can understand the meaning of the mentalistic notion of a concept.

As we saw, Positivists construed the task of science as explaining and predicting phenomena in nature via laws. From a Positivist's perspective, then, we need to see if cognitive scientists have been able to come up with hypotheses about the behavior of concepts. One hypothesis that has been offered by a number of cognitive scientists is that concepts are stored in the mind as prototypical instances and a metric in terms of which new instances are compared to the prototype. Thinking involves bringing this concept into working memory and formally manipulating it in some rule governed way. The hypothetico–deductive method requires that once such a hypothesis is advanced, a variety of consequences must be derived from it that can be tested. One prediction is that subjects should be slower in making judgments about less typical instances of a category than more typical instances since they would be further from the prototype, a result that is confirmed by the data of Rosch (Rosch, 1975; Rosch & Mervis, 1975)[5] and others (see Smith & Medin, 1981, for a review). A further prediction is that there will be higher agreement between subjects when asked to judge whether objects closer to the prototype are members of a category than those further away. This result is also borne out (e.g., McCloskey & Glucksberg, 1978). From a Positivist's perspective, at this point the hypothesis has been supported by tests, but it has not yet been taken up into a general, axiomatizable theory. But one can anticipate the kind of theory that the Positivists' account of science would envision. Researchers would need to embed the idea of prototype and metric into a general theory of the structure of the cognitive system so that the idea of concepts being encoded as prototypes with a metric would be a derivable consequence.[6]

It does seem reasonably easy to take instances of work in cognitive science, such as the work on concepts and categories, and explicate it using the Positivists' account of what a science is. On the surface, the Positivist's account seems to offer a compelling account of the character of scientific explanations. Despite its initial force, I noted in the course of this chapter some problems that confronted the full articulation of this view. During Positivism's heyday many felt that these could be resolved and we would then have a clear account of the nature of scientific inquiry that could justify the claim of science to provide knowledge of nature. In recent decades, however, this optimism has waned. Although some philosophers remain convinced that the basic picture of science offered by the Positivists is correct, many have found the objections to be fatal and have begun to look for alternatives. In the next chapter I begin to examine the criticisms that have been raised against Logical Positivism, whereas in chapter 4 I discuss alternatives to the Positivist conception.

---

[5] Rosch (1978) explicitly disavows the idea that her data should support the claim that concepts are stored in terms of prototypes and metrics, although many psychologists have so interpreted her.

[6] For a quite different perspective on the significance of this work on concepts and categorization, see chapter 6.

3

Challenges
to Logical Positivism

INTRODUCTION: CHALLENGES TO SPECIFIC
THESES OF LOGICAL POSITIVISM

One of the virtues of Logical Positivism is that it is a view of scientific explanation that is articulated in clearly stated, specific doctrines. This enabled careful analysis and criticism. The result has been a number of objections that have focused on specific doctrines. These criticisms served to chisel away at the foundations of Positivism, and subsequently there have been broader criticisms that attack the program as a whole and recommend replacing it with a quite different approach to philosophy of science. In this chapter I look at a number of the more specific objections, reserving for the next chapter an examination of the major alternative approaches to philosophy of science that have been advocated in recent decades.

THE ATTACK ON CONFIRMATION

One of the first major challenges emerged from Karl Popper, a philosopher who was often in dialogue with members of the Vienna Circle and who was viewed by them as a friendly critic. Like the paradoxes of confirmation discussed in the previous chapter, Popper's criticisms focused on the hypo-thetico–deductive model of a hypothesis development and testing. The Positivists, as I noted, were aware that they could not solve the problem of induction, but thought that at least positive tests of a hypothesis could give support to that hypothesis. Popper (1935/1959 and 1965) contended that this assumption was false. Just as Hume had shown that it was never possible to prove that a general statement was true, Popper maintained that one could not even show that it was likely to be true. The degree of support we could offer to a general statement was always dependent on the few cases we could examine. If we treat our degree of confirmation of a general claim as a probability measured by the proportion of all cases that we have actually examined and that have turned out positive, we could never establish that a general hypothesis had greater than a very small probability of being universally true.

Popper proposed a radical remedy to this problem. He recommended abandoning the whole endeavor of seeking well-confirmed theories, and proposed instead that scientists focus on demonstrating that some hypotheses are false. His reason for making this shift was that although there is no valid deductive or even good inductive form of reasoning from which we could derive a general proposition from specific instances, there is a valid argument form according to which we can show that evidence disproves an hypothesis. This form is *modus tollens* or denying the consequent:

$$\text{If } H, \text{ then } P$$
$$\underline{\text{Not } P}$$
$$\text{Therefore, not } H.[1]$$

If H is the hypothesis in question and P is a prediction that follows from it, then when P turns out to be false we can infer that H is false.

Popper went on from this simple logical point to propose a general schema for scientific inquiry. Empirical investigation, he proposed, should attempt to disprove hypotheses. Although this sounds defeatist, Popper has tried to show how it could be the basis of a constructive enterprise, which could result in continual improvement in the accuracy of our science. He characterizes his program as one of conjectures and refutations. A scientist should begin by making conjectures about how the world is and then seek to disprove them. If the hypothesis is disproved, then it should be discarded. If, on the other hand, a scientist tries diligently to disprove a hypothesis, and fails, the hypothesis gains in stature. Although failure to disprove does not amount to confirmation of the hypothesis and does not show that it is true or even likely to be true, Popper speaks of such an hypothesis as *corroborated*. The virtue of a corroborated hypothesis is that it is at least a candidate for being

---

[1] If we tried to create a similar argument to confirm a hypothesis, we end up with the invalid form of affirming the antecedent:

$$\text{If } H, \text{ then } P$$
$$\underline{P}$$
$$\text{Therefore, } H.$$

See the discussion of logic in chapter 1.

a true theory, whereas hypotheses that have been disproved are not even candidates.

The substitution of the term *corroboration* for *confirmation* is not a mere linguistic change for Popper. It represents a broader change and rejection of other aspects of the Positivists' schema. It signals a rejection of the Positivists' attempt to distinguish meaningful from meaningless discourse through the verificationist theory of meaning. Popper substitutes a quite different program of demarcation—one that demarcates scientific from nonscientific discourse in terms of the risk that true scientific theories face of being wrong. In taking the risk of being wrong, the theory is, according to Popper (1965, chapter 1), "forbidding" certain things to happen. That is to say, if the theory is true, then certain things cannot happen. If they do happen, then the theory was not true. This ability to forbid certain things is what gives scientific theories their power, for they distinguish things that are possible if the theory is true from those that are not. The more things the theory rules out, the more powerful the theory. We can speak of it as more informative—it is telling us that, of the circumstances that we otherwise think might be possible, only this limited subset is actually possible. Thus, the more the theory rules out, for Popper, the stronger the theory actually is, for it tells us more about how the world actually is.

Although Popper intends to apply this thesis primarily to theoretical statements, we can illustrate his point with a straightforward, observational claim. There are a variety of conditions that could make the sentence "It is sunny today" false. The truth of the sentence thus informs us that those circumstances that would make the sentence false do not occur. Thus, an informative sentence rules out possible configurations of the world and a highly informative sentence rules out large numbers of ways the world might be. In contrast, a sentence that is certain or almost certain to be true ("It is either sunny or not sunny today") rules out little and so tells us little about how the world really is.

To apply this view to theoretical statements, Popper appeals to the testability of scientific theories. True scientific theories are ones that can be put to critical tests where we can specify in advance what would count against the theory. An example Popper used was the test of Einstein's general theory of relativity, which predicted that light from stars would be distorted in a particular way when the light passed near to the sun. This can only be tested during an eclipse, and Popper greatly admired Eddington's test of Einstein's theory during such an eclipse. Because the prediction was risky it was quite conceivable that it would come out false. On the other hand, Popper found Freudian and Adlerian psychology to be incapable of such tests because both theories could be applied to any possible circumstance that arose. Hence, for Popper, they were not informative, and hence not true scientific theories even if they are meaningful by the canons of the Positivists.

In the process of conjecture and refutation, Popper recommends starting with our current theories. Some of these have passed all tests to date, whereas others have failed one or more tests. These latter theories present problems to the theorist, and the theorist's task is to propose new theories that solve these problems.[2] Popper then imposes three kinds of constraints on such new theories, two of which focus on the theories themselves, while the third focuses on the results of testing the theories. Popper (1965) requires first that the "new theory should proceed from some *simple, new, and powerful, unifying idea* about some connection or relation (such as gravitational attraction) between hitherto unconnected things (such as planets and apples) or facts (such as inertial and gravitational mass) or new 'theoretical entities' (such as field and particles)" (p. 241). The reason for this requirement is that the goal of theorizing is to get at basic features of nature and not merely to posit ad hoc relations so as to solve problems with previous theories. The second requirement is that the new theory should be independently testable, by which Popper means that it should have new testable implications that have not been previously investigated. Here is where the theory must be bold and risky. Moreover, it is as a result of possessing such implications that the theory promises to tell us something new.

A theory will tell us something new even if its new implications are proven false, because we will have learned new empirical findings that future theories must accommodate. But Popper places a third requirement on a good theory: It must pass some of these new, severe tests. The reason is that progress would be stifled if we continued to offer new theories without them passing at least some of these new tests. For one thing, if the new tests constantly turned out negative, we would no longer have any clear idea at what points the theory was in accord with nature and where it was making new, risky proposals. Thus, we would lose the ability to devise crucial tests that could distinguish true from false theories. A crucial test involves finding a situation where a theory that generally fits the natural world can be precisely compared to it in a well-defined circumstance so that a specific piece of the theory could be falsified or further corroborated. Such tests, however they turn out, give us precise information, but they are not possible unless our theories are, for the most part, accommodating our experience.

What the process of conjectures and refutations offers, for Popper, is a means of continually homing in on the truth. We are able to reject ideas that turn out false and use theories that continue to be corroborated. Although

---

[2] Popper acknowledges that the problems to be solved might not stem simply from empirical falsifications of previous theories, but may be theoretical problems involving how to unify two theories or dispense with seemingly ad hoc principles in current theories. This interest in theoretical problems is developed much more fully by Laudan, whom I discuss in chapter 4.

such corroboration does not give us a logical basis for increasing our confidence that the hypothesis will not be falsified on the next test, it does serve to limit us to an ever narrowing set of hypotheses that might be true. Popper has compared this process to natural selection, for both nonadapted organisms and false theories are weeded out, leaving the stronger to continue in the competition. But Popper points to an important difference. If we are maladapted to our environment, it is we who perish, but if our theories are maladapted, we can let them perish while we pursue better theories. Popper thus speaks of letting our theories die in our stead. (Other theorists have pursued the idea that theory development may be parallel to the process of evolution by natural selection. See, for example, Campbell, 1974a; Toulmin, 1972.)

The implications of Popper's falsificationism for disciplines in cognitive science are rather serious. There are cases in cognitive psychology, for instance, where competing theories do make contrasting empirical claims. For example, Sternberg (1966) compared three different models of how humans might access items stored in memory. Each model predicted a different pattern of reaction times, so Sternberg had subjects memorize a list of numbers and then asked them to identify whether particular numbers were on the list. The experiment thus pitted these models against each other so that those models that did not fit the reaction time data could be rejected.[3] However, it is widely recognized that many theories in cognitive psychology and linguistics, and most simulations in artificial intelligence, fail to accommodate the data already available. It is not necessary for them to make radical new predictions in order to be tested and possibly falsified, for they are clearly already falsified. On Popper's grounds, these theories should be rejected.

The problem, for cognitive science, is that it is very difficult to create theories to accommodate existing evidence. Perhaps, however, what is at fault is Popper's claim that the only way to advance science is by conjectures and refutations, not the practice of cognitive science. This is suggested by some of the psychology of reasoning studies. Taking a lead from Popper, some early studies[4] focused on the fact that humans do not rigorously try to falsify

---

[3] The three models were that (a) the mind viewed all the numbers at once to determine if the number was on the list; (b) it searched the numbers sequentially and stopped when it reached the queried number to report a positive result and reported a negative result when there were no more numbers on the list; and (c) it searched the list sequentially, but reported neither a positive nor a negative result until it reached the end of the list. The first two models were rejected on the basis of reaction times, whereas only the third, rather counterintuitive, model was corroborated.

[4] One study performed by Wason and Johnson-Laird (1972) asked subjects to try to figure out the rule that lies behind the sequence 2, 4, 6. The rule might be something general like "any three positive whole numbers." The subjects are encouraged to offer additional sequences to test their possible rules before announcing them. Typically subjects begin by assuming the rule is "three sequential even numbers." Rather than trying to falsify this hypothesis by offering

hypothesis, but rather mistakenly go about seeking confirming data. Other studies (see Mynatt, Doherty, & Tweney, 1978) suggest, however, that seeking confirmatory data for early hypotheses may be quite reasonable in a variety of problem environments where the character of the environment and the nature of the problem are not well understood. It may be necessary to acquire some concrete data and structure plausible models before it makes sense to engage in rigorous falsification. The research endeavors in many parts of cognitive science may be at just such a state where exploratory, non-falsificationist research is required.

Regardless of these difficulties in applying Popper's falsificationism to current cognitive science, it is important to note how his approach to philosophy of science marks a significant break with the picture of science offered by Logical Positivism. In giving up the quest for highly confirmed theories, Popper also foregoes the program of building an ever larger theoretical structure of well-confirmed propositions. Rather, he directs science to make new, bold conjectures that correct for previous failings rather than amplifying and rendering more adequate a theory already supported by a number of confirmations. Thus, he begins to undercut the cumulative conception of science that emerges from Logical Positivism and opens up a concern with how science changes. On the other hand, there are still affinities between Popper's conception of science and that of the Positivists. Although he draws different consequences from the use of logic, and does not present axiomatization as the goal of theorizing, he still holds that modern logic can provide a framework for analyzing scientific investigation and that scientific investigation is to be grounded in empirical inquiry. For example, the focus is still on the context of justification, not discovery, and explanation still involves deriving a fact from a law and a set of initial conditions.

---

a sequence like "3, 2, 1," however, they try to confirm it by offering sequences like "8, 10, 12." Incidentally, this problem can be used to create a useful simulation of the scientific process. This can be done by letting a group represent members of a scientific community competing for the Nobel Prize, with one person (e.g., a teacher) playing Mother Nature. Any member of the group can perform an "experiment" by offering up a sequence, to which Mother Nature gives the "result" by saying "Yes" (e.g., it fits the rule) or "No." Any member of the group can also publish a hypothesized law by asserting it. As in real science, Mother Nature does not say whether the law is right or wrong, but leaves that to be determined by other members of the group through further experiments. The simulation ends when the group chooses someone to receive the prize. During the simulation, both the laws and experimental results may be written on a blackboard so that after the simulation the participants can go back through the events sequentially and discuss the strategies that seem to be at work at each stage in the problem solving activity. One thing that can be pointed out at the end of the simulation is that the rule that the group ends up with may not be the "right" one (i .e., the one Mother Nature was using). In science, even after the Nobel Prize is awarded, it is still possible that we will learn that the hypothesis is wrong.

REPUDIATION OF THE DEDUCTIVE-
NOMOLOGICAL MODEL OF EXPLANATION

Although both the Positivists and Popper accepted the correctness of the deductive–nomological model of explanation, it has been criticized by numerous philosophers. These critics contend that something other than deduction from laws and statements of initial conditions is required of explanation. Two alternative views have emerged; one of them requires that an explanation identify a cause for the event being explained, whereas the other treats explanation as a matter of answering certain kinds of questions. On both of these views, it is claimed that an event may be explained even if a description of it has not been derived from more basic laws.

The appeal to causes as explanations is partially motivated by dissatisfaction with the treatment of statistical explanation within the Positivists' framework. I noted previously that the Positivists attempted to generalize the D–N model to handle statistical explanation by holding that in a statistical explanation it is possible to derive a statement that the event in question is likely to occur. One objection to this approach is that it only works with events with greater than .5 probability. It does not allow us to explain relatively low probability events, such as getting cancer after a lifetime of smoking. But often the goal is to explain low probability events. Salmon (1970, 1984) contends that if we view explanation as a matter of identifying causes, we can handle such situations very naturally. He proposes that commonly we identify such causes by a process of *screening off*. To explain the idea of screening off he offers an analogy to a situation where we might be trying to find the source of light. If we can find a place where we can put a screen to cut off the light, then we have identified where the light is coming from. Generalizing, his idea is that if we can identify a way of interrupting an effect, we have found the causal chain. That which we have interrupted can be taken to be part of the causal chain and we can continue up the causal chain until we find the source that generates the causal chain.

The idea of screening off works equally well in probabilistic situations as in deterministic situations. If we have a situation where the effect (for example, a disease) is found in 10% of the population, and we take action that interrupts the causal pathway, then we will reduce the percentage of the population in which the effect occurs. We will then be able to identify the cause which led to 10% of the population initially suffering the disease. Moreover, this idea also works with partial causes. If we do not reduce the percentage to 0, but only to 5%, then we can infer that we have interrupted one of the causal pathways but not all. To capture what is happening in situations of these kinds, Salmon introduces the idea of statistical relevance. With unrelated events, the probability of both events occurring together is simply the product of the probability of each occurring. When the probability of both events occurring together is greater than the product of each occurring, then Salmon speaks of the two events being statistically relevant to each other. An example of such statistical relevance is given in the case of smoking. The probability of being a smoker and dying prior to age 70 is greater than the probability of death prior to age 70 times the probability of being a smoker. In such cases, Salmon maintains, either one event is the cause of the other, or both are effects of a common cause. Once we identify the existence of a common cause situation, we can use techniques like screening off to find this common cause.

One factor that is particularly noteworthy about Salmon's approach to explanation is that explanation does not involve a deduction of a statement of the event to be explained, as the Positivists had maintained. Explanation is not a relation between laws and statements of events at all; rather, it is an answer to a "why" question that cites the event or entity that is causally responsible for the phenomenon. (In offering this view, Salmon rejects the Positivists' approach of examining only the language of science. Instead, Salmon directs his attention to the events in the world and their causal interactions.) Salmon's approach to explanation also differs from the Positivists in giving a central role to causation. In the Positivists' account, the concept of cause had no special status and one might well explain an event without knowing its cause. Some laws invoked in explanations might state causal relationships, but that was not required. In fact, the Positivists had no resources for distinguishing causal laws from other generalizations embedded in the axiomatic structure of a theory. By focusing on procedures whereby one can interrupt causal chains, Salmon proposes to identify causal relations and allow them to assume a central place in an account of explanation.

The second alternative to the D–N model begins by focusing on the context in which people seek explanations. Both Bromberger (1968) and Scriven (1962) contend that explanation begins when someone asks a question because he or she is missing some information. What counts as an explanation will depend on what information the person is lacking. For example, a person may ask why a certain window broke. What the person may not know is that it was hit by a baseball. In this case, telling the person what hit the window will suffice for an explanation. In other contexts, the person may know that the window was hit by a baseball, but will want to know why being hit by a baseball led to the window's breaking. Then the person will be seeking information about the structure of windows that explains why they break when hit with certain kinds of objects whereas other objects do not cause breakage.

One result of placing the issue of explanation in this context of answering questions is that giving an explanation may not always be the same kind of activity. Asking for an explanation may involve asking for quite different things in different contexts. Sometimes it may be a request for a scientific theory and a theoretical account about how things happen, but not always. Sometimes it may be a request for an identification of an unknown cause. In general, however, the critics maintain that when a person asks for an explanation, the person does not require a derivation of a description of the event from a general law and a statement of initial conditions. It is here that the break with the Positivists appears, for they held that one did not have an explanation if one did not have the deductive structure. The Positivists did acknowledge that when, in practice, a scientist is asked for an explanation, he or she might not provide the whole deductive account, but only part of it. This, however, they viewed as a matter of shorthand, believing that to explicate the character of the explanation, one had to offer the whole deductive structure. The critics contend, however, that such a deductive structure need not be present even implicitly in an adequate explanation.

Bromberger and Scriven make a similar point about theoretical explanation. For the Positivists, a theoretical explanation involved development of an axiomatic structure in which the particular law was derived from more basic axioms. Both Bromberger and Scriven contend that even when the questioner asks for a theoretical account, the request may not be for an axiomatic structure. In fact, often producing such an axiomatic structure will leave the questioner asking for further explanation. The person may be able to handle the derivation within the axiomatic structure and still not feel that he or she understands the event. To explain the event to this person may require providing a model of the phenomenon in question so that the person can see how different factors, as described by the equations in the axiomatized theory, interact with one another.

In some disciplines of cognitive science (e.g., linguistics) there are large theoretical structures that can be viewed as giving explanations comparable to D–N explanations. The computer programs that underlie cognitive simulations may also have sufficient logical structure that it may be plausible to view them as subsuming the behavior to be explained under laws in a D–N style. But in other disciplines relevant to cognitive science, such as cognitive psychology, the explanatory endeavors are often far more modest. Researchers do not have elaborated theories from which they can derive specific behaviors once given initial conditions. Rather, a particular aspect of behavior is noted, and researchers try to identify a factor that might explain it. For example, Tulving's (1983) distinction between an episodic memory system (devoted to memory for particular events) and a semantic memory system (devoted to memory for general propositions such as those about the meanings of language or general facts about the world) can be viewed as part of an attempt to explain different sorts of results that can be produced on various memory tasks. The theory is not presented axiomatically in a full set of laws from which particular events are presented, but much more informally by describing the differences in the two proposed memory systems and then showing that these differences would account for the different results on memory tasks for the two kinds of memory. What Tulving did, then, can be seen as an attempt to isolate a potential causal factor that affects memory behavior without creating a D–N structure for deriving statements of memory behavior from general laws and statements of initial conditions. Insofar as Tulving's work is fairly typical of explanatory endeavors of cognitive psychologists, these endeavors might be better understood from the perspective of the critics of the D–N model, rather than trying to force them into the structure of D–N explanations.

These challenges to the deductive–nomological model have reduced the desire of some philosophers to construe all explanations as deductive and all scientific theories as objects to be axiomatized in the manner of Euclidean geometry. However, they have also led to a situation where there is no clear and widely accepted model of what a law or theory is or how they are to figure in explanation. The core of the Positivists' view of science has been attacked, but there is no general agreement on a replacement. But, as I show next, even more basic assumptions upon which the Positivists' view was built have been brought under attack, suggesting that the kind of philosophical enterprise in which they were engaged is misguided.

CRITIQUE OF THE ANALYTIC–SYNTHETIC DISTINCTION

In the previous chapter we saw that in applying the verificationist theory of meaning the Logical Positivists invoked *analytic statements*. These statements often are characterized as statements that are true in virtue of the meanings of the words contained in them. Hence they are not dependent upon evidence. In this respect they are distinguished from *synthetic statements* that make substantive empirical claims for which evidence is appropriate. The distinction between analytic and synthetic statements was fundamental to the Positivists' enterprise and indeed to much of analytic philosophy, which has tried to resolve philosophical problems by analyzing the meanings of important concepts. In addition to analytic sentences that spelled out the meaning of theoretical sentences, the Logical Positivists were also concerned with two other classes of analytic propositions—mathematical propositions and logical propositions. Because the truth of these statements could be secured independently of experience, they could be used in developing a science, or in articulating the philosophical foundations of science, without any risk of introducing error. Thus, as we have seen, the Positivists freely employed symbolic logic in their analysis of science, assuming that these logical underpinnings were not themselves dependent for their truth upon the substantive empirical claims of the science.

In the early 1950s, however, W. V. O. Quine launched an attack on the distinction between analytic statements and synthetic statements that has had quite broad ramifications both for philosophy of science and analytic philosophy generally. Quine's strategy is to show that the term *analyticity* can only be defined in terms of other concepts like *meaning*, which in turn can only be defined in terms of analyticity. The result is a vicious circularity. Thus, terms like *analyticity* and *meaning* fail to meet the Positivists' own standard of meaningfulness according to which only terms which have clear standards for verification count as meaningful (see the first section of chapter 2). Quine's (1953/1961b) conclusion is that insisting on a distinction between analytic statements and other statements in any language, formal or natural, is "an unempirical dogma of empiricists, a metaphysical article of faith" (p. 37).

Quine draws upon this rejection of the analytic–synthetic distinction to launch a full attack on the general program of the verificationist theory of meaning. He treats the assumption that all sentences of a language should be reduced individually to experience as a second unempirical dogma of empiricism and proposes to replace it with a view according to which "our statements about the external world face the tribunal of sense experience not individually but only as a corporate body" (p. 41). He contends that the terms of our language are interconnected with one another in a vast network, so that we cannot differentiate between those connections in the network that establish the meanings of theoretical terms from those that present empirical findings.

The conclusion Quine draws from this is quite startling and revolutionary. It goes far beyond attacking just the verificationist theory of meaning. He contends that we must give up the idea that we can use experience either to confirm or to falsify particular scientific hypotheses. When experience contradicts our science, we must modify our science, but Quine's contention is that we can do this in a wide variety of ways. We can always protect particular hypotheses by modifying others. For example, if someone who believes that only humans can use languages is confronted with the reports of primate linguistic capacity, he or she can either take these reports as refuting evidence or narrow the conception of language so as to protect the original claim. Without a fixed analysis of meaning, the fundamental idea of either confirming or falsifying scientific hypothesis on the basis of evidence is called into question. (This claim that evidence does not itself determine our evaluation of hypotheses is commonly referred to as the "Quine-Duhem thesis" since the physicist Pierre Duhem, 1906/1954, had advanced a similar claim a half century earlier.)

As I noted in the previous chapter, the concept of an operational definition was an extension of the Positivist's verificationist theory of meaning. The demand to define terms operationally has been prominent in the social sciences, including psychology. One benefit of this demand has been to tie psychological theorizing to experimental results and avoid speculative theorizing that borders on meaninglessness. But if Quine's challenge is correct, then these operational definitions must be viewed in a different light than they commonly are. They should not be taken as specifications of meaning that are absolute and unmodifiable, but rather they should be seen as synthetic claims, subject to revision in the course of inquiry. That is, when a theoretical claim is jeopardized by an experimental result that is based upon operational definitions of theoretical terms, one option that should be considered is revising the operational definition to save the theoretical claim. One result of opening this option is that judgments about theoretical claims will not be precisely determined by experimental results in the manner that seemed possible given the use of operational definitions, but Quine would maintain that this kind of ambiguity is something we must accept, and not try to legislate against.

One consequence of Quine's attack on the analytic–synthetic distinction is that decisions about modifying scientific claims must be treated as pragmatic, not logical decisions. A further result is that, in deciding where to modify our theoretical structure in the face of negative evidence, we may choose to modify the propositions of logic and mathematics as well as those more generally thought of as part of empirical science. Thus, these principles lack the privileged status that the Logical Positivists assumed they possessed. Quine acknowledges that typically we will be loath to modify the principles of logic, but he claims this is not due to any privileged status they enjoy. The reason is rather that they are so "central" to our network of scientific claims that modifying them will have enormous consequences throughout our science and our conceptual systems generally. Thus, it is the pragmatic principle of conservatism, not privileged status, that explains why we find rejecting the principles of logic and mathematics nearly inconceivable.

The consequence of depriving logic of any privileged status, however, is enormous. The Positivists' program is built on the assumption that logical analysis is inviolable and that philosophical analyses that depended on logic alone could not therefore be supported with empirical investigation. Without such a foundation, philosophy loses its claim to be able to inform us simply through the vehicle of logical analysis. In light of this, Quine claims that we must forego any hope for a "first philosophy" that is independent of and established prior to experience. Rather, we must treat philosophical discussions of science as themselves a part of empirical inquiry (Quine, 1969b, 1975). Thus, Quine advocates a "naturalized epistemology" that is integrated with work in psychology. (For Quine, however, this psychology is to be behavioristic, not cognitive. See Bechtel, in press a, chapter 3.) As part of psychology, philosophical claims about how we can have knowledge of the world and how science can produce knowledge are just as open to revision as any part of science.

Needless to say, Quine's arguments have not been universally endorsed by analytic philosophers whose *modus operandi* is challenged by these arguments (see Grice & Strawson, 1956; Katz, 1964; Putnam, 1962). However, a number of philosophers have taken Quine's challenge to heart and have come to accept a need to base philosophical analysis on empirical findings. A generation of philosophers of science have accepted the importance of studying both the history of science and contemporary science and to develop accounts of science that fit the actual mode of scientific inquiry. One cost of working within such a naturalized framework is that these philosophers can no longer claim to be strictly normative, prescribing how science ought to be done if it is to have logical validity. Instead, they must settle for being pragmatic commentators on science, explicating what is revealed by empirical inquiries about science and making pragmatic recommendations as to how scientists might learn from their past practices and better realize their objectives.

A CHALLENGE
TO THE OBSERVATION–THEORY DISTINCTION

Yet another critical assumption made by the Positivists was that through empirical experience we had an objective basis for evaluating scientific claims. Such empirical experience was acquired through observation. Because the Positivists characterized the evidence relationship in terms of relations between sentences, they required that the evidence acquired from experience be coded in a set of sentences. This set of sentences had to be distinct from the set of sentences stating the laws or theories to be tested so that they could be appealed to in the course of such tests. Quine's attack on the analytic-synthetic distinction began to call this assumption into question, for he challenged the idea that we could clearly differentiate between the empirical claims of a science and the meanings of the terms used to present these claims. He proposed that science constituted a network that could be adjusted at various points, with no point being privileged. Yet, Quine remained sympathetic to the basic empiricist view that our theories of nature must be grounded in sensory experience and he offered criteria to differentiate a class of observation sentences from the theoretical networks built upon them. These sentences, he claimed, could provide a neutral basis for testing different theoretical claims. However, the assumption that there is an objective set of observations that are neutral between theories has increasingly come under attack as a number of authors have argued that observation itself is theory-laden.

One of the strongest proponents of the theory-ladenness position was Hanson (1958), who maintained that what we perceive is influenced by what we know, believe, or are familiar with. He offered examples where we directly perceive certain objects that would not have been recognized at all by members of previous generations because they were unfamiliar with such objects. A simple contemporary example would be a microcomputer, which all of us recognize immediately but which would have been unrecognizable to anyone 50 years ago. We directly see microcomputers because of the background knowledge we bring to the perceptual context. When Hanson argues that we *directly* perceive such objects, he is rejecting the claim that we are seeing a neutrally characterizable object and then making an inference about what the object is. Sometimes we do make inferences based on what we see, but this is not the usual situation when we see ordinary objects or even special laboratory objects with which we are familiar. Rather, we see what our knowledge and training equips us to see. Hanson's position here is, by now, one quite congenial to many cognitive scientists who argue for some degree of top-down processing through which knowledge enters into observation. In the classical experimental paradigm, the stimulus is presented in a situation where contextual information directs subjects to one particular interpretation of the stimulus, even though others were possible. For example, in the display in Fig. 3.1, the middle letters of the two words are drawn identically, but nearly everyone sees the first as an "H" and the second as an "A".[5]

THE CAT

FIG. 3.1.   The middle letter in each word is printed the same and without context would be ambiguous. In context, however, it is viewed as an "H" in the first word and an "A" in the second (figure after Selfridge, 1955).

For Hanson, part of what is involved in learning a particular science is learning to see the world in a particular way. Hanson proposes that the difference between the trained observer and the untrained observer is similar to the gestalt shifts that any of us can experience when we look at ambiguous figures. Figure 3.2 provides a classic example. Many of you can see both an old woman and a young woman in this figure. But you cannot see both figures at the same time. Looking at it one way you see it *as* a young woman, looking at it in a different manner you see it *as* an old woman. The expression "see it as" suggests that you are making an inference, but this is what Hanson resists. We do not see the figure neutrally as a set of lines and then infer that one curve represents the nose, and so forth. To see the figure as a set

---

[5] Hanson, however, would resist the temptation to characterize the information processing that goes into recognizing objects in terms of inferences and problem solving.

of lines in fact takes sophisticated training, which most of us lack. Rather, we see the figure of the young woman or the old woman.[6]

FIG. 3.2.   An ambiguous figure that can be seen either as an old woman facing forwards and to the left or as young women looking away to the left. (figure after Boring, 1930).

Hanson, however, recognized that the consequences of this view for the Positivists' conception of science are quite serious. It shows that observation does not offer a neutral basis for evaluating theoretical frameworks, but is itself influenced by the theoretical framework a scientist brings to the situation. Those who bring different theoretical frameworks to the same situation will see the world differently. Hanson points to the example of Tycho Brahe (who still believed in a form of earth-centered astronomy) and Copernicus (who introduced the sun-centered astronomy) viewing a sunrise. Tycho, according to Hanson, sees the sun rising, whereas Copernicus sees the earth turning toward the sun. Recognizing such evidence involves, he claims, being trained to see certain features of the world in a certain way (i.e., in accord with a particular theory). This is even true in naturalistic settings, such as in the observations of Tycho and Copernicus, where no sophisticated experimental equipment is employed. It arises even when one is not adjudicating between competing theories. It would arise in a situation where a therapist had to evaluate whether a particular mode of therapy has changed a person's behavior. This requires the ability to identify the behavior and recognize specific changes in it, something a lay person may be ill equipped to do. But the influence of theories is even more clear in the case of experiments involving elaborate equipment to report the data. The tracing on an EKG machine will be immediately recognized and understood in terms of heart

---

[6] The difficulty with the inference proposal can be appreciated when you try to help someone who cannot see the figure in one of the alternative ways and you try to point out features. Although that may help, it does not guarantee success. For many years I could not see the young woman, although numerous people had tried to point out the features. Then in frustration I threw a copy of the diagram upside down in front of a colleague and demanded to know again where this obscure image was. As the drawing hit the table, the picture of the young woman clearly came into view—I simply saw her, I did not infer anything.

activity by a trained technician whereas it will just be a pattern of lines to the lay person.

This challenge to the theory–observation distinction has consequences for cognitive science as well. The data for cognitive science is generally assumed to be behavior. The task of theories is to account for this behavior. Behavior is taken to be something relatively objective, against which we can test the implications of different theories about how the mind works. But the theory-ladenness objection maintains that behavior is not so clearly objective. How we classify behavior may depend upon the theory we are using to try to understand the behavior. We can capture part of the difficulty by considering how we might distinguish between action and mere bodily movement. For a cognitivist, this distinction presumably depends on the mental states we are attributing to the person. If we attribute appropriate desires and beliefs to a person, then the act of raising an arm may appear to be an action—something done in order to achieve the desire. But if we have a quite different theory about what is going on in the person's head, the same bodily movement may be ascribed a quite different significance, either as part of a different action, or as mere behavior that is not itself an action. Although such difficulties are most serious when dealing cross-culturally, where we lack an appropriate understanding of the cognitive perspective of the other person, it arises also in standard experimental designs. A common problem is to determine how the subject understood the task he or she was performing. Given a different understanding of the task, the behavior of the subject, which provides our observational evidence, may be appropriately described much differently.

The claim that all perception is theory-laden has been viewed by some philosophers (Scheffler, 1967; Shapere, 1966) as having grave implications for the appraisal of science. They have portrayed it as undercutting objectivity and rendering science totally subjective. The objectivity is undercut by the fact that we must already accept part of the theory in order to make the requisite observations (e.g. , we must accept the classification of behavior or the theory behind the EKG machine in the examples in the previous paragraph). If we lack an objective, theory–neutral reference point, it is claimed, scientists who hold competing theories will simply see what they are prepared to see by their theory and there will be no theory-free reference point to which we can refer to settle disputes.

These fears are, however, almost certainly exaggerated. Those who hold that all perception is theory-laden are not discounting that the stimuli from the external world play a critical role in determining what we see. These stimuli are factors constraining perception and mark a critical difference between imagination and perception. Theory-ladenness does not entail that we can see whatever we want to. Given the way we have been trained to see, what we see is determined by what is there to be seen. For example, given that we has been trained to read an EKG machine, we read the pattern that is there. We may see things that go against our theories and be forced to revise them. For example, you may have formed an hypothesis that on a particular reaction time measure two tasks would require identical times. When you carry out the experiment, however, you may find that the reaction times for one task are reliably longer than those for another. Then (ignoring the problem raised by the Quine-Duhem thesis) you will need to revise your theories.

When you revise your theories in light of experience, these theories may lead you to carry out different kinds of observations. You may develop different apparatus and use different techniques for reporting what you observe. Once again, however, nature may not fully cooperate, What you see may not correspond to what you expect even though the way you see is influenced by your theory. Nature may contravene your expectations, forcing yet another revision in the theory. Thus, even if observation is theory-laden, it is possible to discover that your theory is wrong. Theory-ladenness does not render science totally subjective, as the critics of theory-ladenness seem to fear. Objectivity remains because it is still possible (and happens frequently) that we make observations that contradict our theoretical predictions and thus show us that our theories are wrong.

This is not to say that the theory-ladenness of observation does not produce real problems. These problems arise when those who use different theoretical perspectives try to produce evidence to show the other that their way of interpreting the world is correct. Such people may well disagree about what it is they see and both may take what they see to support their theory. In such a case, without a neutral set of observations, it may not be possible to adjudicate between competing theoretical disputes simply on observational grounds. This, however, may not be too severe a problem if there are other ways of settling such disputes. A potentially more serious difficulty is that one may even lack ways of comparing competing theoretical frameworks. For the Positivists, the observational framework provides a basis for explicating the meaning of scientific claims, and if there is no common observational framework, such comparisons between competing frameworks may not be possible. This problem is commonly referred to as the *incommensurability of theories*. The incommensurability problem has been developed by those philosophers who have focused on the historical development of science, to which I turn in the next chapter. There I show how these philosophers view the theory-ladenness of observation as just a piece of a story that ultimately requires us to adopt a quite different view of science.

OVERVIEW OF THE CRITICISMS
OF POSITIVISM

In this chapter I discussed four basic objections that have been raised against

Positivism. The Positivists sometimes adopted the metaphor of a science as an architectural structure built up from its foundations. I have presented these criticisms in an order that takes the structure apart from the top. The second and third sections reviewed objections that attack the superstructure—the hypothetico–deductive method of theory development, the deductive–nomo-logical model of explanation, and the axiomatic view of theories. The objec-tions discussed in the last two sections focused on the foundational assumptions of the verificationist theory of meaning and the idea of a neutral foundation in observation. (For further discussion of these and other criticisms of Logical Positivism, see Suppe, 1977, and Brown, 1979.) Altogether, the criticisms sketched in this chapter have proven so destructive that only a few contemporary philosophers still affirm allegiance to the Positivists' position in its original form.[7] Yet, the Positivists' picture of science remains the most comprehensive we have. The failure of Logical Positivism, if indeed it has failed, is, therefore, all the more noble and it leaves a legacy. Most philosophers of science find it impossible to dispense totally with the Positivist heritage even while recognizing various shortcomings. In the following chapter, however, I describe an alternative approach to philosophy of science that seems to many philosophers to provide the beginnings of an alternative.

---

[7] One important element of the positivists' tradition, a focus on a formal analysis of science, however, is affirmed by a number of contemporary philosophers. Prominent examples include the development of the semantic view of theories by Van Fraassen (1980) and defended by Giere (1979), Lloyd (1984), and others; a variety of probabilistic interpretations of science, many deriving from Bayes Theorem (Levi, 1967); and Glymour's (1980) bootstrapping analysis.

4

Post-Positivist
Philosophy of Science

THE EMERGENCE OF HISTORICALLY GROUNDED
PHILOSOPHY OF SCIENCE

The most influential development in philosophy of science in the wake of the demise of Logical Positivism has been the introduction of an historical perspective into Philosophical thinking about science. This has resulted from a greater concern among philosophers of science to describe the actual character of scientific investigation and the ways in which scientists choose which theories to accept or at least to pursue in further research. Within the framework of the Positivists and most of their critics (Popper being a notable exception), it was generally accepted that the primary factor that should govern decisions about the acceptability of a theory was the degree to which it corresponded to the evidence.[1] Post-Positivist philosophers argue,

---

[1] Even the Positivists recognized that this was not a sufficient criterion. In principle, at least, theories are always *underdetermined* by the evidence. There are always a variety of possible theories that will accommodate any set of evidence. This, however, is not a terribly serious problem for practicing scientists because it is often very difficult to find even one theory that perfectly fits the evidence available. But even then there is an important underdetermination in science. When theories fail, there are a variety of ways to revise the theoretical framework to accommodate the apparently disconfirming evidence. The Positivists and their descendants have proposed a number of criteria for guiding such decisions. Quine and Ullian (1970), for example, propose five such criteria—conservatism, modesty, simplicity, generality, and refutability. According to these criteria, we should prefer new theories that require the least change in currently accepted views, that are least risky in their claims, that are most simple, but yet that have broad generality and for which it is conceivable to acquire falsifying evidence. Although recognizing some tension between their criteria, they argue for each in terms of how following them is likely to enhance our ability to develop true theories.

however, that these are not the primary factors governing scientists' decisions and that, by focusing on them, earlier philosophers have developed accounts of science that do not accurately describe real science. If philosophy of science is to be of any value, it must attend to those factors that govern real scientific practice and that have enabled science to become a valuable knowledge producing enterprise.

Having criticized the Positivists for failing to describe real science, post-Positivist philosophers of science propose to develop their analyses not from general logical considerations but on the basis of careful examinations of the actual processes of science, particularly as revealed through its history. This, however, gives rise to a crucial issue. By showing how theories could be logically justified or corroborated on the basis of objective evidence, the Positivists hoped to show why science was able to produce true accounts of nature and why it should be valued as an objective source of knowledge. Further, the Positivists offered their account as a normative guide for the conduct of good science. By focusing on how scientists actually make decisions and countenancing factors other than criteria that could improve the likelihood of giving true accounts, advocates of an historical approach seem to be foregoing any possibility of producing a normative account of science and are left with attempting to provide only a descriptive account.

Historically based philosophy of science also encounters objections from another direction. A number of contemporary historians and sociologists of science claim that their tools of analysis enable them to provide a more adequate descriptive account of how science actually operates than philosophers. In particular, they charge that philosophers are preoccupied with the reasons scientists give and the logic of their arguments, but that these are not the true determinants of scientific investigations. Rather, these historians and sociologists maintain that a variety of institutional and social factors are what really govern the conduct of science. This raises the issue of whether there is a distinctive task for philosophy of science once it surrenders its claim to being able to give, on the basis of logical analysis, a normative account of what science should be.

Many philosophers have tried to show that there is still a point to analyzing the reasoning of science and to addressing such questions as how science makes progress. In doing so, they recognize that social and historical factors do influence the actual process of science, but they maintain that the reasoning of scientists is also an important determinant. Some post-Positivist philosophers even hold that their endeavor may give rise to normative judgments about the best ways to pursue scientific inquiry. They maintain, however, that judgments cannot be grounded on a priori principles but must be pragmatic judgments based on what has been successful science.

The primary inspiration for the development of post-Positivist philosophy of science, as well as for many of the recent endeavors in the history and sociology of science, was the publication of Thomas Kuhn's (1962/1970) *Structure of Scientific Revolutions*. This book, although not establishing a new general theory of science, offered a radically new framework for thinking about the character of science. Hence, the first part of this chapter is devoted to an exposition of Kuhn's account of science. I then survey more recent developments within this general approach.

KUHN'S CHALLENGE: NORMAL AND REVOLUTIONARY SCIENCE

Kuhn challenged the assumption of many previous philosophers of science that science offered a steadily accumulating body of knowledge. In contrast, he claimed that scientific disciplines go through distinct stages and that the character of research in the discipline varies between stages. Kuhn differentiates five stages: (a) immature science, (b) normal mature science, (c) crisis science, (d) revolutionary science, (e) resolution, which is followed by a return to normal science. Thus, a closed loop results involving stages b, c, d, and e (see Fig. 4.1).

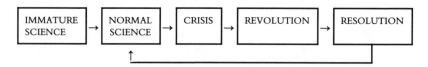

FIG. 4.1.   Five stages in the history of scientific disciplines according to Kuhn.

Following the lead of the title of Kuhn's book, much of the discussion has focused on scientific revolutions. However, some of the most revolutionary claims Kuhn makes concern not revolutionary science but what he labels "normal science." Thus, I begin with his conception of normal science.

Normal science requires the establishment of what Kuhn has called variously a "paradigm" or "theoretical matrix." In his original book, Kuhn was not precise in his characterization of paradigms, which has resulted in numerous publications in which Kuhn and others (see Kuhn, 1970b) have tried to clarify that notion. The intuitive idea underlying Kuhn's term *paradigm*, however, can be explicated readily. A paradigm provides a framework for characterizing phenomena that a particular discipline takes as its subject matter. This might involve a basic model or a general theory. Kuhn has in mind items like Copernicus' model of the planets revolving around the sun or the theory of physical bodies attracting one another in accord with Newton's laws. In cognitive science, the idea of the mind as an information-processing system could constitute the paradigm.

A paradigm is not simply a model or a theory, but also includes instructions as to how such a theory or model is to be developed and applied in further research. These instructions may take the form of examples showing how derivations are to be made from the theories in the manner espoused by the Positivists, but they need not be so restricted. In describing these instructions, Kuhn appeals to science textbooks. The general theories of a discipline are commonly taught through a set of examples that show how to apply the theory to phenomena in its domain. For example, a textbook may illustrate Newton's principles by showing how they can be used to determine the gravitational attraction the earth exerts on a body on its surface. The examples taught often are the first applications that were developed in the discipline using the theory and they become the models for the new students. In cognitive psychology, the example could be the experiments used to establish the distinction between short-term and long-term memory and the use of chunking to explain how experts appear to exceed the normal limits on information in short-term memory. Kuhn refers to these standard applications of the basic framework as *exemplars*. (He also speaks of these exemplars themselves as *paradigms*, using the term now in a narrower sense.) One important function of an exemplar is to teach students by providing a model for them to imitate. Students begin by literally imitating the exemplar itself, for example by solving the same equation for different values. Later they learn to modify and extend the exemplar to solve new problems by analogy to the original problem solution.

Even though I have used the term *theory* to characterize one aspect of Kuhnian paradigms, Kuhn's understanding of theories is quite different from that of the Positivists or their critics considered so far. A theory need not be something that can be rendered into an axiomatic structure. It is not a set of postulates from which observations are deduced. Rather, it often consists in a rather fuzzy schema of how nature behaves—a schema that is imprecise and requires a great deal of further clarification (as does the idea that cognition involves processing information). Moreover, Kuhn offers a quite different account of how theories figure in the research of normal science than did the Positivists or Popper. A scientist's goal, according to Kuhn, is neither to confirm nor to falsify theories. Rather, it is to fit the theory to nature. The initial theory is incomplete. It offers a general account of how processes in nature work, but this general account needs to be embellished and filled in. Normal science must figure out what must be added to the general account so as to apply it to specific situations. This may involve figuring out ways of performing measurements in specific contexts or it may involve supplying additional assumptions that are needed to cover those contexts. Practitioners of normal science are continuing to do what they learned to do as students—imitate the exemplars they learned in school in new contexts. Through such activity they extend the applicability of the general theory or paradigm.

The process of further developing the paradigm by applying it to new cases is not necessarily an easy task. The historical record, Kuhn claims, shows that theories seldom fit nature precisely. Even during the period in which a particular theory or paradigm (e.g., Newtonian mechanics) is used and generally accepted, there are predictions that are not borne out in observations. During normal science these differences between theoretical predictions and empirical observations are not taken as falsifying the theory, but rather as creating further problems scientists must solve. Sometimes when the theory fails to fit nature the researcher will tinker with the theory, but that is not the only recourse. Kuhn contends that generally when experiments do not come out in accord with a theory, the problem is attributed to the experiments and not to the theory. The task of the experimenter, according to Kuhn, is to get experiments to produce results in accord with the accepted theory. In this endeavor, the theory is assumed to be largely correct and the task is to make it work. The success of a scientist during a period of normal science is judged in terms of whether he or she is able to resolve problems or puzzles that result from experimental failures and to demonstrate new applications of the already accepted theory. Thus, we see a key difference between Kuhn's conception of science and that of the Positivists. For the Positivists the task of science was to evaluate theories whereas for Kuhn it is to work out the details and develop experimental applications of theories.

Because of the nature of the task during normal science, the activities are clearly delineated and success is easily evaluated. The result is that there is general agreement and harmony within the scientific community. Such agreement and harmony is a sign for Kuhn that the community is engaged in normal science and that a paradigm is in place. Prior to the acceptance of such a paradigm, such agreement will be rare. Activities will not be guided by a generally accepted paradigm. Rather, there will be competing schools, each with its own view of how the discipline should develop and each trying to establish hegemony over the discipline for its approach. Such conflict between schools characterizes Kuhn's first period, the period of *immature science*. According to Kuhn, many of the social sciences are still in this kind of period, waiting for the first paradigm to be established. Rather than setting out to make the paradigm work, researchers spend most of their time battling over what general approach should be adopted. It is only once such a paradigm is established that the discipline will start to make progress because progress involves fitting an already accepted paradigm to nature. (The battles between various schools of psychoanalysis give a clear model of what Kuhn has in mind. Experimental psychology was presumably in this situation at the end of the 19th century, when associationists, functionalists, and structuralists all propounded their vision of what the science of psychology should be like.)

It is not necessary for researchers to prove that their paradigm is correct in order to reach the stage of normal science. Rather, a paradigm is adopted because it seems to offer potential for explaining a particular domain of phenomena and suggests a research program that various scientists can work on together. Probably the first clear case of normal science in psychology emerged with the rise of behaviorism. Although it began as simply another school, it offered a variety of techniques (e.g., classical conditioning, later operant conditioning) and an agenda (to show how much of behavior could be accounted for by behavioral laws) that generated a sustained attempt to force nature to conform to the mold of the paradigm.

Although generally such paradigms exhibit significant successes at the outset, Kuhn maintains that most paradigms eventually reach a juncture where unsolved problems begin to build up and success in solving problems slows significantly. Instead of new solved problems, failures, or what Kuhn calls "anomalies," begin to occur. This produces the third of Kuhn's stages, the stage of *crisis*. In response to the reduced rate of progress and the amassing of unsolved problems, the rules of research that are generated during the period in which the paradigm was successful are relaxed and researchers become more imaginative in considering ways in which the paradigm itself may have to be modified. Thus, to continue with the example of behaviorism, after its initial successes there emerged a variety of problems in which researchers were interested but which seemed beyond the reach of behaviorist explanations. These included language, rational planning, and problem solving. Skinner's (1957) *Verbal Behavior*, although intended to extend the behaviorist program into the domain of language, convinced many others of the poverty of the behaviorist approach. Behaviorism was then in the crisis period.

Sometimes the imagination shown during a scientific crisis will, Kuhn claims, result in the development of new, alternative paradigms that work with different fundamental principles and models and offer their own promise of creating a problem-solving tradition. If such new paradigms begin to develop, the discipline enters Kuhn's period of *revolutionary science*. The use of the political term *revolution* is clearly intended by Kuhn. A revolution is a period of active struggle between defenders of the old paradigm and the proponents of the new one. As in a political revolution, the rules that govern during normal times are no longer applicable (for these rules depended on the paradigm that is now under assault) and so part of what is at issue is what rules will be used to decide between the opposing paradigms. It is here that Kuhn makes his most contentious claims. He contends that competing paradigms are incommensurable in that they cannot be compared and evaluated on rational grounds.

In arguing for incommensurability, Kuhn draws upon the claimed theory-ladenness of observation discussed in the previous chapter. In accord with Hanson, Kuhn denies that there is a neutral observation language and claims that practitioners of a paradigm learn to report their observations in a theory-laden (or paradigm-laden) manner. Because each paradigm will have its own way of reporting observations, advocates of competing paradigms will not characterize what they see in the world in the same way. At one juncture Kuhn speaks of scientists working from different paradigms as living in different worlds. Kuhn also concurs with Quine (see previous chapter) in repudiating the analytic–synthetic distinction and the idea that vocabulary of a language can be assigned meanings independent of the theories presented in the language. Hence, for Kuhn there is no neutral language in which one can compare paradigms. The result is that the competing parties in a scientific revolution must resort to extra-rational means to settle their dispute. Fundamentally, this involves the proponents of one paradigm convincing significant numbers of scientists to adopt their paradigm.

During the revolution, researchers return to a situation much like that found in immature science. Practitioners of competing programs bicker amongst themselves just like the proponents of different schools do in an immature science. Thus, in the late 1950s and through the 1960s there were active debates between behaviorists and those advocating the new cognitivist approach (for examples of the cognitivists' attacks, see Chomsky, 1959 and Miller, Galanter, & Pribram, 1960). The two groups waged bitter arguments about the legitimacy of positing mental states and using them in the course of explanations. Behaviorists and cognitivists defined the goal of psychology differently and offered different criteria as to what would constitute an adequate psychological explanation. Given the nature of these differences, they could not be resolved in the same manner as differences would be resolved in normal science, for there was no agreement on what counted as an adequate psychological explanation. That, in fact, was what was in dispute. Eventually cognitivists generally gained the ascendancy, largely by attracting new researchers to their approach and showing that a successful research program was possible. In some departments behaviorists remained prominent and carried on their research, whereas other behaviorists quietly adopted some elements of the cognitivist approach. Overall, however, cognitivism supplanted behaviorism.

What has happened accords with Kuhn's characterization of the typical outcome of a revolution—a new group of researchers has gained ascendancy (controls the awarding of degrees, access to journals, etc.). It has pushed its paradigm on the discipline and created a new period of normal science. This process is typical of what occurs in Kuhn's final stage of *resolution* during which one school succeeds in making its paradigm dominant. The resolution generates a new period of normal science and a repeat of the cycle. There is some evidence that the cycle is about to repeat again in cognitive science. Cognitive scientists who take the name "new connectionists" have pointed out shortcomings in the traditional cognitivists' program and the past few years have witnessed vocal and sometimes acrimonious debates between traditional cognitivists and new connectionists. The emergence of connectionist research programs suggest that the alternative paradigm is developing and may succeed in developing its own normal science.

Kuhn's claim that competing paradigms are incommensurable so that scientific revolutions can only be settled through extra rational means has been the focal point of much subsequent controversy (see Gutting, 1980; Scheffler, 1967; Shapere, 1966). The reason is obvious—Kuhn's account seems to undermine the validity of science as a rational enterprise. Instead of basing the acceptance of a paradigm or theory on good rational justification (i.e., on sound logical arguments), Kuhn's view is that the decision to accept a paradigm is a matter of taste or persuasion. Kuhn does offer one extra-paradigmatic criterion for evaluating paradigms—their progressiveness. He characterizes scientists as choosing a paradigm because of its potential to solve puzzles and extend its range of applicability. But many philosophers have found this to be inadequate. If using different paradigms results in such drastic differences as Kuhn portrays, the puzzles confronted by two paradigms will not be the same. The identity of problems will be paradigm bound. More drastically, we will not even be able to determine when two paradigms are competing in the same domain because they will offer radically different accounts of the domain for which they are a paradigm.[2] As we see, this is one of the issues that many post-Kuhnian philosophers of science have tried to address.

Through his account of normal science and revolutionary science Kuhn has transformed philosophical thinking about science, but has not succeeded in creating a new orthodoxy. He refocused philosophical thinking on the actual dynamics of scientific activities and away from the abstract logic of confirmation and falsification of scientific theories. Kuhn's accounts have opened up a new kind of criticism of philosophical theorizing—a criticism that charges that the philosophical theory in question does not accurately reflect the processes that govern actual scientific investigation. Such a charge has been leveled against Kuhn's own theory by philosophers who have followed in his footsteps and tried to study the actual dynamics of scientific investigations. Although I cannot hope to discuss all the competing views put forward since Kuhn, I highlight some of the points where these views have differed from Kuhn's so as to reveal the character of contemporary thinking about the nature of the scientific enterprise.

---

[2] In the case of cognitive psychology and behaviorism, there is a case to be made that the two enterprises are not really concerned with the same thing and should not be viewed as competitors. Behaviorism is concerned to identify the external factors governing behavior while cognitivism is concerned with the mediating structures inside the mind. One could readily grant that both are important and look for ways to incorporate insights from both approaches (see Bechtel, in press b; Schnaitter, 1987).

FEYERABEND'S ATTACK ON METHOD

Although most of Kuhn's critics have objected that he sacrificed too much of the rational or logical character of science in his account of how paradigms succeed each other in revolutions, at least one critic, Paul Feyerabend, has pushed to an even more radical position. In his earlier writings (Feyerabend, 1962, 1963a, 1965) he argued against two features of Positivistic philosophy of science that he calls the *consistency condition* and the *condition of meaning invariance*. The consistency condition holds that new theories should be consistent with currently held theories. The condition of meaning invariance holds that the meanings of terms should be held constant across theories (e.g., by something like the verificationist theory of meaning). Feyerabend's objections to these two conditions rest on examination of actual scientific practice and on demonstrations that cases of major advance in science have not adhered to them. For example, Newton's laws often are portrayed as subsuming Galileo's law of free fall and Kepler's law of planetary motion, but Feyerabend argues that Newton's law is actually inconsistent with both of them (e.g., Galileo posits a constant rate of acceleration in free fall, whereas Newton's laws predict a decreasing acceleration). To make his argument against meaning invariance, Feyerabend argues first that the meaning of terms depends on the theoretical context in which they are used, and then shows that critical terms (e.g., mass) change their meaning from one theory (Newton's) to another (Einstein's). Both the consistency principle and the condition of meaning invariance impose, Feyerabend contends, a destructive conservatism on science that would paralyze it.

Feyerabend finds an unhealthy conservatism built into any attempt to specify a methodology for science. In particular, he rejects the idea that researchers should continue to accept a theory until it has been falsified. He contends that we need to consider alternative theories in order to discover the data that might falsify a theory. Each theory we pursue will bring to light new data, and it is these data that may serve to falsify our preceding theories. Again, Feyerabend argues through examples, pointing to the example of Brownian motion, which would not have been discovered simply by those trying to test the second law of phenomenological thermodynamics. It was only discovered by those investigating the kinetic theory of gases, which is inconsistent with the phenomenological second law (Feyerabend, 1965). Feyerabend thus rejects Kuhn's view of normal science, claiming both that such periods of research done totally within the framework of a single paradigm are not common in science and that they would be destructive of science. Science, Feyerabend contends, must depend on maintaining a plurality of pursuits.

Having rejected both Positivist and Kuhnian accounts of scientific methodology, Feyerabend (1970, 1975), advanced a principle of *methodological anar-*

chism that denies that there are any sound methodological principles that should be imposed on science. He claims that any principle we might propose has been violated by good scientists and had to be violated for science to progress. He (1970) concludes that "there is only one principle that can be defended under all circumstances, and in all stages of human development. It is the principle: *anything goes*" (p. 22). Although in many other respects, Feyerabend aligns himself with Popper, in this he challenges Popper as well, arguing that we must even pursue theories that have been amply falsified. Pursuing even these falsified theories may reveal new information, which may serve to invalidate the supposedly falsifying data. In particular, he maintains that new theories will, almost inevitably, be falsified by data produced by older theories but may themselves reveal new data which favors them. In order to break the hegemony of old theories, and bring new data to light that may in turn defeat those theories and support the new idea, Feyerabend calls upon scientists to proceed "counterinductively." This involves producing and defending theories that seem already to have been effectively refuted by current evidence. His contention is that it has been the rule violators who have made the most progress.

To defend counterinduction, Feyerabend points to Galileo, whom he portrays as succeeding only by sabotaging the enterprise of the dominant Aristotelian physics through effective propaganda and circular arguments. When Galileo first offered his new theories of motion, the Aristotelian establishment could readily offer counterevidence. For example, against the theory that the earth was in motion it was seemingly sufficient to drop an object and note that it fell directly to the spot below it, not to a spot behind, as it would if the earth had moved during the fall. To undercut this evidence, Galileo had to argue circularly. The circular arguments would employ unorthodox research methods to establish unorthodox theoretical claims and then use those results to justify the use of the methods themselves. For example, Galileo sought to provide evidence for the new Copernican astronomy according to which the earth orbited the sun. One of the keys to his claim was the assertion that celestial bodies like the moon were in fact physical objects like the earth. To establish this he invoked the telescope, through which one could detect the mountainous lunar landscape. However, the Aristotelians dismissed the use of the telescope on the grounds that when it was used to look into the heavens it would produce distortions because of the quite different etherial medium through which light was passing. So Galileo had to invoke a new optical theory. Only by packaging his alternative view as a whole and then insisting on answering all objections on grounds internal to his new conception, was Galileo able to establish his new physics.

On the basis of such historical analyses, Feyerabend contends that attempts to prescribe particular methodologies for scientific research are used primarily to protect vested interests and to prevent new approaches from developing.

He warns against attempting to devise rational criteria for deciding between theories, including criteria that appeal to how progressive a theory has been and seems likely to be in the future. New ideas that have not had a chance to devise their own methods of support need to be protected against premature dismissal. He even maintains that we should hold on to long-tried ideas that have failed, such as alchemy, because we can never tell when these old ideas might produce new insight and show us errors in our current theories. Feyerabend carries this point to what many would consider an extreme. He maintains that any account, no matter how absurd it seems to those who think in terms of contemporary science (he cites creationism, astrology, and parapsychology), might prove instructive.

Generally, Feyerabend's views have been deemed too extreme to be worth serious treatment, and so he has lost credibility. Yet, he has provided a useful service in showing how conservative established science can be, and how generally recognized progress in science sometimes requires going outside the established order. Most philosophers, however, are interested in what rational strategies are available to maximize scientists' endeavors to improve their science. Hence, unlike Feyerabend, most post-Kuhnian philosophers of science have tried to show how rational considerations can provide useful guidance.

LAKATOSIAN RESEARCH PROGRAMMES

In trying to explicate how science is a rational enterprise, a number of philosophers, who generally accept the importance of adopting an historical perspective, have sought to bring logical analysis back into the philosophy of science and to rekindle some of the same interests that inspired the Logical Positivists—that of evaluating and justifying the scientific enterprise. This is clearly seen in the work of Lakatos (1970, 1978) who analyzes cases from the history of science, but freely adopts the Positivists' strategy of reconstructing these episodes so as to show how they could have progressed by adhering to rational canons. He argues that for philosophical purposes we can overlook some of the details about how a science actually progressed and develop an alternative account about how it could have progressed in a rational manner.[3] Unlike the Positivists, however, Lakatos is interested in both discovery and justification, and, in particular, in the ways in which a science may develop over time. Lakatos' account of the character of science can thus be seen as an attempt to recast Kuhn's insights about the nature of actual science as an historical process into a perspective that can explicate its rational import.

---

[3] This approach of Lakatos' has aroused the wrath of a number of historians and sociologists of science, and has been disavowed by many subsequent philosophers of science.

Lakatos begins by taking issue with Kuhn's claim that we can differentiate distinct stages of normal and revolutionary science. Rather, Lakatos contends that science is seldom dominated by just one paradigm, as Kuhn claims in his account of normal science, but rather that competition between paradigms generally co-occurs with processes of development within a paradigm. Lakatos also takes issue with Kuhn's conception of normal science as filling in and further applying a single paradigm. He contends that research often consists in developing a succession of theories, in which new theories replace older ones while preserving important features of the older theories. To allow for this idea of a succession of theories, Lakatos replaces Kuhn's term *paradigm* with the term *research programme*. The common thread linking different theories into a common research programme is a "hard core" of basic assumptions shared by all investigators. This core is surrounded by a "protective belt" of auxiliary assumptions. The hard core, which may consist of assumptions such as "No action at a distance," remains intact as long as the research programme continues, but researchers can change the auxiliary assumptions in the protective belt to accommodate evidence that either has accumulated or is developed in the course of research.

For Lakatos, the ultimate measure of a research program is whether it is progressive. Progress consists in developing new theories in the protective belt around the core. Lakatos distinguishes two kinds of progress—theoretical and empirical progress. *Theoretical progress* consists in extending the empirical scope of a theory by applying it to new empirical domains. *Empirical progress* consists in corroborating empirically the new claims that are made in the course of theoretical progress. (In these notions of theoretical and empirical progress we can see the influence of Popperian principles on Lakatos' thinking.) To be counted as progressive, the research tradition must be making both theoretical and empirical progress, although Lakatos allows that the empirical progress may be more intermittent than theoretical progress. If it is not progressing, Lakatos speaks of the research programme as degenerating. Unlike Popper, however, Lakatos does not see degeneration, even when the new theories in the research tradition seem to be falsified, as providing a reason to give up the research programme. A verdict that a research programme is degenerating is not final and should not, Lakatos maintains, lead to the total rejection of the degenerating research programme. A programme may be very progressive for a period, degenerate for a while, and return as a progressive programme again. Within cognitive science, connectionism might be such a research tradition which, after languishing, has once again become progressive. In the guise of perceptrons (Rosenblatt, 1962) and Hebb's (1949) account of reverberation of activation in neural networks, the connectionist model initially seemed to offer great hope. Partly as a result of criticisms (e.g., Minsky & Papert's, 1969, criticism of the perceptron model) and partly due to lack of major successes, the connectionist model languished until it was rekindled in the current connectionist literature. Now once again the connectionist program seems to be advancing due to enhancements in the types of models used, and connectionists are developing models that give realistic performance on numerous cognitive tasks.

For Lakatos, the way a research programme makes progress is not totally random but is guided by heuristics. He distinguishes negative and positive heuristics. The negative heuristic of a programme is simply the injunction not to modify the core principles of the program. More significant is the positive heuristic, which "consists of a partially articulated set of suggestions or hints on how to change, develop the 'refutable variants' of the research programme, [and] how to modify, sophisticate, the 'refutable protective belt' " (Lakatos, 1970, p. 135). These heuristics play a critical role in the development of a research programme, for they are what determine whether a research programme will be progressive. In successful research programmes, these heuristics will enjoy a period of success as they guide researchers to the development of viable new theories, but almost inevitably they will become exhausted. Then the programme slips into degeneracy, although it may revive when someone develops new heuristics to restart the programme or finds a way to graft the old programme onto a new endeavor that itself is progressing. Such a graft may not be totally consistent, as the assumptions of the new and old theories may disagree. If, however, the graft suggests ways of solving problems within the old research programme, the inconsistency will not be critical.

Lakatos' conceptions of science brings together Popperian considerations about what makes scientific investigation rational with the Kuhnian perspective of looking at larger scale units as the effective units in scientific progress. One of Lakatos' important insights, which constitutes a departure from Popper in the direction of Feyerabend, is to recognize that in its early days a new research programme will not yet have achieved as much success as older programmes. Moreover, given the initial, simplified version of the early theories offered in the programme, there will be many phenomena that seem to falsify them, but that subsequent theories in the program will nonetheless be able to handle if they are allowed to develop. Thus, Lakatos contends that new research programmes, which show potential, need protection at the outset until they have an opportunity to develop. From Lakatos' perspective, both early cognitivism and contemporary connectionism can claim a grace period before they should be expected to compete as equals with the preceding research programmes.

By rejecting Kuhn's notion of normal science as involving the dominance of just one research program and proposing that competing research programmes are always being pursued, Lakatos introduces a new kind of theory evaluation—a relative evaluation as to which research programme is best. For Lakatos, the measure is progress, measured in terms of extending the theoretical and empirical scope of the theories in the program. One of the more interesting developments in the wake of Lakatos' work is an attempt to develop a more complete account of what such progress consists in and how it can be measured.

LAUDAN'S RESEARCH TRADITIONS

Laudan (1977) proposes an account of scientific activities designed to capture some of the strengths of Kuhn's and Lakatos' account and yet overcome shortcomings in them. Laudan agrees with Kuhn and Lakatos that the main activity of scientists is problem solving. But he offers a more complete account of the kinds of problems scientists encounter and also a finer grained analysis of how scientists may evaluate the seriousness of problems and the importance of problem solutions. In developing his account of science as problem solving, Laudan invokes the idea of a large-scale unit in science that he calls a "research tradition." Like Lakatos' research programmes, research traditions for Laudan consist of a sequence of theories, but they lack a common core that is immune to revision. What holds a research tradition together are simply common ontological assumptions about the nature of the world and methodological principles about how to revise theories and develop new theories.

Laudan distinguishes two kinds of problems that can confront a research tradition—empirical inadequacies of the current theories and conceptual problems with the theories comprising the tradition. Laudan's treatment of empirical problems is generally consistent with that of Kuhn and Lakatos—scientists face empirical problems when expectations based on the theories within their research tradition fail. It is by introducing conceptual problems as important kinds of problems driving scientific research that Laudan claims to be making a new contribution. Conceptual problems do not result from failure of empirical fit, for they could arise even if the theories were totally adequate empirically. The simplest kind of conceptual problem would be an inconsistency within a theory or an inconsistency between two theories that are conjoined in the research tradition. But Laudan claims that there are other sorts of theoretical problems as well: inconsistent ontological assumptions; conflicts between expressed ontological views and theories; and conflicts between the claims of theories and the broader world views of society, including religious or political views. Laudan has in mind such conflicts as those between the assumption that light is a unitary phenomena and the light-wave duality thesis, and those between evolutionary theory and religious fundamentalism. For cognitive science, such a problem might be the tension created by assuming that the mind is an information processing machine that works by deterministic principles and moral principles that seem to require free will.

Laudan not only broadens our conception of what counts as a problem that a research tradition must address, but also tries to develop a finer grained analysis of what problems are important to solve. Although any empirical or theoretical problem would, in principle, be worth solving, many are set aside as less important. Empirical problems, he proposes, are evaluated in terms of how important a challenge they seem offer to the research tradition and whether other competing research traditions have been able to solve them. Consider the case of an anomalous empirical finding that neither results from explicit tests of major theoretical assumptions nor has been explained by any other research tradition. This does not pose nearly as serious a problem as a research finding that directly confutes a major tenet of the research tradition and has already by accounted for by theories in a competing tradition. Conceptual problems can range from a serious problem as when there is a clear logical inconsistency between two accepted propositions, to a moderate problem when it seems implausible that two accepted propositions case are actually both true, to a relatively minor problem when two logically consistent propositions fail to support each other in a way that might be desired.

The task of scientists is to solve both the empirical and conceptual problems they encounter. In this effort it becomes important for them to evaluate competing research traditions. The capacity for such evaluation is what makes science rational. Like Lakatos, Laudan argues that the basis for evaluation is the progressiveness of the tradition. But just as Laudan broadens the conception of what counts as a problem, he also proposes that there are different standards one may use to measure progress in different contexts. One context is where we have to take practical action, for example, to use the results of scientific investigations in treating a disease. Here it is the overall progress that has been made by the research tradition that is relevant. However, when deciding what research tradition is likely to bear the most fruits in the future (e.g., in deciding which one to fund) we will be concerned with the promise of the tradition to solve future problems. We may use as a guide how rapidly research is progressing in the tradition, and choose a tradition which has not solved as many problems as another but is making rapid progress over one that was previously very successful but seems now to be making little progress. Thus, Laudan maintains that we might accept one research tradition to guide our actions while pursuing another in our research.

There is a distinctive aspect of Laudan's account of science that I have not yet touched on. Most of the philosophers who have adopted a historical perspective on science and who have concerned themselves with the progressiveness of science have assumed that science is progressing toward a true conception of nature. Laudan, however, although employing the idea of progress, does not think science is getting any closer to the truth. He argues for this partly by observing how frequently scientists have repudiated previous theories and replaced them with others that are radically different. He denies that there is any metric upon which we can evaluate later theories as being closer to the truth than earlier ones or judge ourselves to be closer to the truth than our predecessors. Laudan maintains that the idea of truth as a goal for scientific investigation is peripheral. Progress is sufficient.

Laudan's account of scientific change, like the others, has attracted critics. On the one hand, insofar as Laudan permits such things as inconsistencies between a particular scientific theory and a religious tradition to matter in evaluating a science, he seems to be allowing nonscientific factors to enter into the evaluation of science. Although it is unproblematic that such external considerations do affect the direction of science, many question whether they should have such a role in a rationally developed science. Laudan however defends using these external considerations in evaluating a research program because he views them as also a part of our cognitive apparatus. He in fact maintains that even in nonscientific domains such as politics and theology the same conception of rationality measured in terms of problem solving applies so that these are equally a part of our rational cognitive endeavor. On the other hand, Laudan has also been attacked for not giving sufficient weight to social factors. Laudan wants to restrict the role played by such social factors in developing science and to emphasize rational considerations. He thus resists the move by some sociologists of science to treat scientific developments as purely social developments and argues for maintaining a privileged role for philosophical analyses of the reasoning of scientists, a contention that many philosophers as well as nonphilosophers regard as problematic.[4] Despite these and other criticisms, Laudan's account at present is one of the most fully developed philosophical analyses of the character of scientific research. Although it does not offer anything as comprehensive or as precise as the positivists' analyses, his analysis of problems and the evaluation of problems offers a promising route to further development.

STUDIES OF SCIENTIFIC DISCOVERY

One consequence of philosophers' growing interest in the history of science has been a growing interest in scientific discovery. As explained in chapter

---

[4] Laudan actually takes an extremely strong position with regard to sociological analyses, arguing that we only need to invoke sociological analyses in cases where analyses in terms of rational decision making fail to explain the behavior of scientists (Laudan, 1981). In part, Laudan is reacting to the "strong program in the sociology of knowledge," which argues that all beliefs, rational as well as irrational, should be explained in the same manner and, because rational factors can never fully determine what should be believed (because of the underdetermination of theories, etc.), social factors are always relevant to explaining scientific practice (see Barnes, 1977; Bloor, 1976, 1981). Not all philosophers have found the strong program inimical to philosophical interests (see Hesse, 1980). There are, moreover, other programs in sociology of science (for example, the laboratory studies of Latour & Woolgar, 1979, and Knoor, 1981, and studies of scientific institutions by Whitley, 1980, 1982) that can be extremely informative for those interested in developing philosophical analyses of scientific decision making.

1, the Logical Positivists made a sharp distinction between the contexts of discovery and of justification. Discovery was assumed to be a nonrational process and so philosophical attention was directed at the question of how theories could be justified, not how they were initially developed. Hanson (1958, 1960, 1967) was one of the first to urge philosophers to redirect attention to discovery. Hanson's own approach, however, constituted only a modest step in the direction of studying discovery. His proposal was to pursue what the 19th century American Pragmatist, Charles Peirce, called *abductive inference*. According to this procedure, you start with a surprising phenomenon, identify the kind of hypothesis (partly on the basis of past experience) that would explain that phenomenon, and then pursue development of that kind of hypothesis.

Hanson's call for studying discovery was answered only gradually. Part of the reason philosophers were reluctant to pursue the study of discovery was that it did not seem to lend itself to logical analysis. Discovery was not a deductive process, because deductive reasoning could only lead one from premises to conclusions that would have to be true when the premises were. Quite clearly there are no such rules that can guarantee that the hypotheses developed in scientific investigations will be correct. Discovery procedures are, at best, fallible. The alternative to deductive reasoning is generally taken to be induction. The most commonly discussed type of induction is enumerative induction in which one proceeds from examples to general statements. (For example, one might, mistakenly, infer from seeing a hundred white swans and no black ones that all swans are white.) But despite Bacon's (1620) claim that such induction could lead to basic theoretical principles, it is generally recognized that such induction cannot generate the kinds of theoretical principles that figure in scientific explanations. For example, it does not lead one to understand the causal processes behind phenomena.

One of the things that has brought about renewed interest in discovery is the recognition, partly motivated by work in empirical psychology, that human reasoning involves additional modes of reasoning than deductive logic and enumerative induction. People invoke strategies of reasoning to deal with problems that may work perfectly well in most contexts, but violate the norms of formal logic. (See papers in Kahneman, Slovic, & Tversky, 1982.) Because scientific reasoning is simply an extension of ordinary human reasoning, there is reason to think that such strategies figure also in science and that a detailed study of the history of science may permit us to identify some of these strategies. (For a useful collection of papers, see Tweney, Doherty, & Mynatt, 1981.)

Simon (Newell, Shaw, & Simon, 1962; Simon, 1980) popularized the idea that in solving complex problems we rely on heuristic principles that simplify the process through which we search for a solution. It is useful to contrast heuristics with algorithms. Although both often can be stated as explicit rules, and so can be implemented in a computer, Wimsatt (1980) identifies three distinctive characteristics of heuristics: (a) they simplify the problem and so are "cost-effective" ways of reaching solutions; (b) they do not guarantee that a solution will be reached, or that the solution arrived at will be correct; and (c) the errors that result will be systematic so that it is possible to devise situations in which any given heuristic will fail. If scientists do reason using heuristics in discovery, then it is reasonable for anyone trying to studying scientific discovery to try to identify the heuristics they use. The systematic errors that result from such heuristics provide a tool for identifying them (see Wimsatt, 1980, for such an attempt to identify heuristics through studying the reasoning of different model builders in population genetics). Moreover, through identifying these heuristics and through identifying the circumstances under which they may fail, philosophers can once again play a normative role of evaluating the practice of science (Bechtel, 1982).

Recently there has been considerable interest by both philosophers and those in artificial intelligence (AI) in using AI as a tool for studying scientific reasoning. Simon and his colleagues have developed a number of programs designed to discover patterns in numerical data (BACON) and certain types of qualitative laws (GLAUBER; Langley, Simon, Bradshaw, & Zytkow, 1987). Currently, Simon is collaborating with an historian of science, Frederic L. Holmes, to develop a program that captures the details of Hans Krebs' discovery of the citric acid cycle in biochemistry. Two philosophers have also made contributions to this endeavor of using AI to understand discovery. Thagard, in collaboration with other cognitive scientists (Holland, Holyoak, Nisbett, & Thagard, 1986), has developed a computer simulation to capture the process through which the wave theory of sound was discovered. Darden, together with Rada (Darden & Rada, in press), has developed a computer program that discovers part-whole relationships (such as the discovery that genes are parts of chromosomes). Darden (1987) and Thagard (in press) both advocate the use of AI reasoning processes as a strategic tool for future studies in philosophy of science. One difficulty confronting this approach is the tremendous diversity of reasoning patterns that are exhibited in cases of scientific discovery. Even if we can develop reasoning strategies that account for particular cases of discovery, there remains a major problem of determining which procedure is appropriate for a particular circumstance. Nonetheless, the introduction of computer simulations into studies of scientific reasoning has introduced a new rigor to the enterprise (because procedures must be explicitly stated) and provided a means of studying these procedures empirically.

Computer simulations are not the only means for studying discovery. A number of philosophers have engaged themselves in the task of trying to extract from cases of science basic principles governing the discovery process. Nickles (1978, 1980a), for example, beginning with Laudan's conception of scientific problems (see preceeding), has explored, through a variety of historical cases, how such problems are constrained by known or accepted information and how these constraints may figure in devising solutions to the problems. (For additional case studies of discovery processes, see the papers in Nickles, 1980b.) One thing that has emerged from these case studies is that the context of discovery is not uniform. Some have argued that there are a variety of stages in scientific discovery, including stages of generation and of pursuit, with different strategies appropriate to each (see Nickles, 1980c, for discussion).

Philosophers have just begun again to study scientific discovery and there is considerable disagreement over how to proceed. Many philosophers remain skeptical that anything of value will result from the endeavor. Others, however, maintain that if philosophy of science is to remain faithful to actual science, then it must develop accurate accounts of a major scientific activity, that of reasoning through problems to new solutions. This is one area where philosophy of science promises to develop in subsequent years and to engage in fruitful collaborations with other disciplines of cognitive science.

SUMMARY OF POST-POSITIVIST
PHILOSOPHY OF SCIENCE

In this chapter I discussed some of the prominent viewpoints developed by philosophers of science since Kuhn's (1962/1970a) publication of *The Structure of Scientific Revolutions*. Although none of these approaches has yet obtained the status once enjoyed by Positivism, they have yielded useful insights into the character of science and have also made philosophers much more concerned with the actual character of scientific research than they were previously. As a result of these analyses, new issues have emerged as principal topics of discussion in the philosophy of science. Shapere (1984), for example, has opened up a new line of inquiry into what the units of scientific investigation are, and has himself argued that the way in which the domain of scientific inquiry is defined is a prominent factor in governing developments in science. Another issue, which is perhaps the most widely discussed current issue, is whether scientific theories must be treated as real descriptions of phenomena in nature, or, in the manner of Laudan, as simply vehicles for characterizing phenomena we experience (see Leplin, 1984; Churchland & Hooker, 1985, for introductions to this debate).

The historical analyses of science that I have focused on in this section have attracted attention from a number of practitioners of cognitive science who have been interested in understanding the development of this field of inquiry. I have already noted that early practitioners of modern cognitive science viewed themselves self-consciously as revolting from the domination of behaviorism and many subsequent writers have used Kuhn's conception of a scientific revolution to characterize the development of the cognitive orientation (Reese & Overton, 1970; Weimer & Palermo, 1973). The development of alternative analyses of scientific development by Lakatos and Laudan, however, has led some investigators to inquire whether the history of psychology and other cognitive sciences might better be characterized using one of these frameworks. Gholson and Barker (1985) argue that Lakatos' account is far more compatible with the history of psychology than Kuhn's. In conformity to Lakatos' views, they argue that the competing traditions of cognitivism and behavioristic learning theory have experienced a long history of competition. One did not simply supercede the other in a Kuhnian revolution. Further, there was interaction between the two traditions, not just competition. As a result, some features of a cognitive perspective were adopted by some researchers in the learning theory tradition while cognitivists themselves made use of some contributions of learning theorists in developing their accounts. Moreover, Gholson and Barker argue that, in conformity with Lakatos' analysis, these research programmes each had periods of progress followed by periods of stasis or degeneracy before becoming progressive again. If one construes late 19th century endeavors by Wundt, James, and others as ancestors of modern cognitivism, one might argue that cognitivism itself was in a period of degeneracy during much of the period when behavioristic analysis dominated, but has reemerged in recent decades as a progressive programme.

Although they see Lakatos as providing a more accurate account of the cognitive sciences than Kuhn, ultimately Gholson and Barker advocate Laudan's approach. A primary advantage they see is that Laudan's account allows for changing core commitments, a phenomenon they attempt to trace through the history of learning theory. They find the idea of a cluster of theories, those held contemporaneously and those held successively, as providing a better account of what actually occurred in the development of psychology. Finally, they argue that conceptual factors as well as empirical factors have shaped psychology, again favoring Laudan's analysis over Lakatos'. For example, in the arguments between behaviorists and cognitivists, much of the controversy revolved around such issues as whether the digital computer provided a useful model of the cognitive system. That issue has recently reemerged with the development of connectionism. One argument advanced for connectionism is that a network system provides a more biologically realistic model of cognition than a digital computer.

These post-Positivist accounts of science do seem to provide convenient tools for explicating developments in a variety of scientific research domains, including cognitive science, but one must be cautious not to view the ease of application as clear evidence of the correctness of one account. At present, there are a variety of competing philosophical accounts of how science works, each of which seem to apply to a number of cases. But to appraise the correctness of any one of these far more rigorous investigations are needed that test philosophical theories against actual history. This process has begun (see Laudan et al., 1986; Laudan, Donovan, & Laudan, in press), but it faces an interesting reflexive problem. In developing historically adequate philosophical analyses of science, philosophers of science have treated their enterprise as itself scientific. Now they face the problem of deciding which model of science to appeal to in adjudicating the battle between competing models of science. For this and other reasons, philosophy of science can still be viewed as a discipline in flux. The post-Positivistic analyses have raised new issues and introduced new ideas that seem potentially fruitful, but as yet there still is no widely accepted, clear understanding of the nature of science.

5

Theory Reduction as a Model for Relating Disciplines

INTRODUCTION: RELATING DISCIPLINES BY RELATING THEORIES

In the last three chapters I focused on the general character of scientific inquiry and scientific theories. I now turn to a more specific issue, the question of how disciplines in science relate or should relate to one another. Many scientists are interested in these questions, but especially those involved in what I term *cross-disciplinary research clusters* such as cognitive science. In these clusters the avowed objective is to integrate contributions of various disciplines to deal with a common problem. One of the last legacies of Logical Positivism has been a very influential model of how to unify disciplines, known as the *Theory Reduction Model*. This model is a natural outgrowth of the Positivist's deductive–nomological model of explanation (see chapter 2). Like other parts of their account, the Positivists' account of reduction is both clear and precise, which partly accounts for its continued influence even after many of the Positivists' doctrines have been rejected. Recently, however, there has been growing dissatisfaction with the theory reduction model and alternative accounts of how to unify science have emerged. In the next chapter, I turn to the points of dissatisfaction with reduction and the attempts to develop alternative perspectives on the relationship between disciplines. In this chapter, however, I focus exclusively on the theory reduction model.

Reduction, like many other terms, carries a special meaning for philosophers. Whereas many scientists employ the term *reduction* for any attempt to invoke the resources of a more basic discipline to explain phenomena belonging to the domain of the higher level discipline (Wimsatt, 1976a, 1976b, 1979), philosophers have focused their account of reduction on the relationship between theories. To avoid confusion, I use the expression *Theory Reduction Model* for the philosophical account. Recall that, for the Positivists, theories were treated as linguistic structures, and that explanation was a matter of deduction. The Positivists treated the relationship between theories in a similar manner, hoping that by focusing on these linguistic structures and the logical relations between them they could avoid potentially tricky questions about how the objects referred to in these theories actually relate (see Churchland, 1986, for a recent defense of this view).

In the following section I characterize the theory reduction model and then turn in subsequent sections to the issue of whether cognitive theories can be related to more basic theories via the Theory Reduction Model. Because theory reduction is concerned with deriving one theory from a more basic one, those using the Theory Reduction Model have concentrated on the relationship between psychology and neuroscience. Thus, that is the predominate example considered in this chapter. In the next chapter, in which I consider alternatives to the Theory Reduction Model, I also consider some other examples of cross disciplinary relationships within cognitive science.

THE THEORY REDUCTION MODEL
AND THE UNITY OF SCIENCE PROGRAM

The Positivists developed the Theory Reduction Model as a vehicle for unifying all of science. The laws of every discipline were to be translated ultimately into the framework of physics and derived from the principles of physics. In this manner all scientific knowledge would be shown to be an application of the principles of physics (see Carnap, 1938).[1]

Behind the Theory Reduction Model lies a conception of nature as consisting of entities at a multiplicity of levels of organization, where entities at any one level are composed of entities from lower levels. Thus, molecules are made up of atoms, cells are in turn made of molecules, and organs are made of cells. (For an alternative analysis of levels of organization in science, see Abrahamsen, 1987.) Various disciplines have evolved to characterize the interactions of entities at specific levels. The theories that seek to characterize phenomena at higher levels, for example, theories about cell behavior, are in fact describing the behavior of entities made up of lower level parts (e.g.,

---

[1] The classical account of the process of Theory Reduction via derivation is found in Nagel, 1961. For this discussion I draw heavily on the account offered by Causey (1977), which in many ways represents the most detailed development of the traditional Theory Reduction Model. See Schaffner (1967) for an alternative.

macromolecules). The behavior of these components are described in terms of lower level theories, for example, those of biochemistry. The task of the theory reduction model is to show how the higher level theories (e.g., those describing cell behavior) might be related logically to lower level theories (e.g., those of biochemistry). Thus, reductionism has a downward orientation because the goal is to relate higher level theories to lower level ones. It is for this reason that the relation of psychology to neuroscience has been of such interest to philosophers.

A problem one faces immediately in developing a Theory Reduction is that higher level and lower level theories use different terminology to describe nature. Before a logical relation can be established between two theories it is necessary to connect the terminology. This requires constructing a translation manual for translating the language in which the higher level theories are written to that in which the lower level theories are stated. The manual consists of a set of rules (generally called *bridge laws*) specifying equivalences between the two vocabularies. Although constructing such translation manuals may seem a rather straightforward endeavor, there is one potentially significant feature of such translation that should be noted. If in fact the same kind of higher level units (e.g., cells) can be made out of different types of lower level constituents (e.g., different macromolecules) then a different bridge law will be required in each instance. I return to this issue later. It also should be noted that the project of translation is itself not a reduction, but a project of limited interest. All it shows is that we can characterize the higher level entities in terms of their lower level composition. It does not show that the higher level laws can be related to those describing lower level behavior.

The main interest in the reductionist program, and its potential for unifying science, arises from a second requirement—that the law statements about higher level entities be derived from the laws developed to explain lower level phenomena. Thus, continuing with the cell example, laws about the behavior of cells (now stated in the language of the lower level and so using terms referring to molecular structures) are to be derived from laws about the behavior of molecules (e.g., the laws of biochemistry). The use of derivation relations is an extension of the Positivists' use of derivation in explanation. Recall that according to the deductive–nomological model of explanation, a phenomenon is explained by deriving a statement describing it from general laws and a statement about initial conditions:

> Law Statement
> Statement of initial conditions
> _____
> Therefore, Statement of phenomenon being explained

The goal in Theory Reduction is quite similar—to derive a law of one science from laws in other sciences. The derivation requires both a statement of the lower level laws and a statement comparable to those specifying initial conditions. These, which are called *boundary conditions*, will detail the particular conditions under which the higher level phenomenon will be produced from the lower level phenomenon. They will specify, for example, the conditions under which chemical events in the cell will result in the phenomenon of meiosis. The complete deduction of the higher level law from the lower level law will therefore have the following general form:

> Lower level Laws (biochemical laws)
> Bridge Laws (relating biochemical terms and cell terms)
> Boundary Conditions (specifying conditions under which
> biochemical events will produce cellular events)
> _____
> Therefore, Higher-level Laws (laws of cell biology)

An often cited example of a successful reduction is the derivation of the Boyle–Charles Law of classical thermodynamics (which describes the relationship of temperature and pressure in an ideal gas) from principles of statistical mechanics. Critical terms in the Boyle–Charles Law, such as *temperature* and *pressure* are identified with terms referring to kinetic properties of the ideal molecules postulated in the mechanical analysis. These equivalences (e.g., of temperature with mean kinetic energy) constitute the bridge laws that enable a translation of the Boyle–Charles Law into the vocabulary of statistical mechanics. Boundary conditions identify the kinds of molecules (e.g., monotonic gas molecules), the container in which their movement is restricted, and the range of temperatures and pressures considered. Given these bridge principles and boundary conditions, the Boyle–Charles Law can be logically derived from the laws of statistical mechanics.

The program of theory reduction often is criticized for ignoring the role of higher level interactions (those involving the interaction of higher level units) which depend on the higher level properties of the units. By giving primacy to lower level laws such as those of biochemistry, reductionists seem to ignore the fact that higher level objects such as cells may have their own characteristics (e.g., motility) that determine how they interact with one another. This objection, however, cannot be made against sophisticated models of theory reduction. Most reductionists are perfectly willing to acknowledge the existence of higher level processes. All they insist upon is being be able to derive the principles governing the behavior of these higher level systems from the laws of the lower level science (given appropriate boundary conditions). Causey (1984) makes this point clear:

> Adequate models for microreductions must take into account the fact that some objects are structured wholes composed of smaller parts that are bonded together in various ways. These structured wholes often have attributes that are not at-

tributes of the individual parts. An adequate microreduction must be capable of describing these attributes of the wholes, and explaining why the wholes have these attributes under specified internal and external conditions. (p. 460; see Hooker, 1981, for a related argument)

One might ask why anyone would be interested in reducing the theory of one discipline to that of another. Advocates of reduction have touted a number of advantages that reduction offers, all stemming from the potential of Theory Reduction to integrate the theories of different disciplines and thus promote unity amongst the sciences. One is that a Theory Reduction simplifies our ontology by showing that certain phenomena that were treated as "basic" by the practitioners of one discipline are really just consequences of other, more basic phenomena. Hence, new basic types of entities or phenomena do not have to be recognized in our scheme of nature. For example, the demonstration that the temperature of a gas is equivalent to mean molecular energy shows that temperature does not have to be treated as an additional basic phenomenon in nature. A similar claim often is cited as a major potential benefit of reducing cognitive theories to neuroscience theories. Behaviorists opposed cognitive theories since they seemed to treat mental events as basic, but if these events can be equated with brain events, then our ontology is simplified and proscriptions against theorizing about mental events can be dropped.

Second, Theory Reduction is taken to provide explanatory unification by offering deeper level explanations of higher level phenomena. We have already seen that the Theory Reduction Model is really an extension of the deductive–nomological model of explanation. The derivation in the reduction can therefore be viewed as an explanation of the laws of the higher level science. The laws of cell biology would be explained by showing them to be consequences of the laws of biochemistry. Similarly, the laws of psychology might be explained if one could show them to be consequences of neuroscience laws. A related benefit frequently cited for Theory Reduction is that it will provide coherence amongst the sciences, thereby increasing the justification for believing the laws of both the reducing and reduced sciences. For example, the fact that the same principles can be used to explain both biochemical and cell phenomena gives us additional reason to think we have the right principles. Similarly, if we can reduce the theories of psychology to those of neuroscience, the support each theory has acquired independently can be shared by the other (see P.S. Churchland, 1986).

Most philosophers who accept the Theory Reduction Model agree that it is not possible to reduce most current psychological theories to current neuroscience theories. This is, however, not a very surprising result. The Theory Reduction Model was designed to deal with completed theories, not with theories still under development. Both psychology and neuroscience

consist of theories that are undergoing development and are not yet sufficiently worked out to permit the derivation of the laws developed in one
discipline from those in the other. This, however, raises the question of
whether the Theory Reduction Model provides an account of a goal toward
which psychology and neuroscience ought to aim. On this question there
are a variety of views, to which I now turn.

ARGUMENTS AGAINST TRYING TO REDUCE
PSYCHOLOGY TO NEUROSCIENCE

One of the most common motivations for opposing reduction is the perception that reducing the theories of one discipline to those of another eliminates
the first discipline. Advocates of reduction often claim that this is a mispercep-
tion because the point of reduction is not to eliminate the reduced discipline,
but to incorporate it within the broader scientific framework (see Churchland,
1986). Nonetheless, there is a sense in which a successful theory reduction
undercuts the status of the discipline whose theory was reduced. It treats the
theories of the reduced discipline (psychology) as just applications of more
basic principles (those of neuroscience). It thereby places the practitioners
of the reduced discipline in the role of applied scientists who are simply working out the applications of more basic principles for specific domains. Thus,
the opponents of reduction fear that if the theories of psychology are ultimately reduced to those of neuroscience, then the role of psychologists is dimin-
ished. Rather than discovering new basic truths about nature, psychologists
would be merely working out the application of theories discovered by
neuroscientists. Because, at least in principle, neuroscience itself would be
capable of providing a full account of psychological phenomena, psychologists
would be performing a redundant task. As I show in the next section, there
are good reasons to reassess this view of the implications of reduction, but
it is a view that has generated much opposition to reductionism.

Finding a position unpalatable is not the same thing as showing that it
is incorrect. A number of philosophers, however, have taken on the additional project of showing that reduction of theories of psychology to those
of neuroscience is not possible. Fodor (1974) tries to do this by arguing that
it is not possible to construct bridge laws equating the terms in psychology
theories with those of neuroscience theories. He contends that although we
use the terms of both theories to refer to the same phenomena in nature, we
cannot equate them. Although the psychological term (e.g., planning for a
vacation) and the neuroscience term (which describes a pattern of neural fir-
ing) may, on a particular occasion, both describe the same state in the brain,
on other occasions these descriptions may refer to different states. The reason
is that the two vocabularies classify things in quite different ways. As an

analogy, consider our terms for color (*blue, red, green*, etc.) and size (*small, large*, etc.). In general, the color classification does not correspond to the size classification (there may be large and small red objects and large and small blue objects) even though all colored objects can also be described in terms of their size. Fodor contends that a similar situation exists between psychological terminology and neuroscience vocabulary. If it does, then there can be no bridge laws between the vocabulary of the two disciplines, and hence we will not be able to carry out the reduction of the laws of one discipline to those of the other.

One commonly mentioned reason for thinking that it is not possible to equate psychological terms and neuroscience ones is that we use the same psychological terms to describe activities in other organisms and artifacts like computers, where we know that the same neural processes are not occurring (see Putnam, 1975a). Fodor also offers other reasons for thinking that such bridge laws between psychology and neuroscience will not be possible. The vocabulary of a discipline is established to state the relationships we are trying to represent in that discipline. Therefore, Fodor contends, psychology and neuroscience are trying to capture different kinds of relationships. This will likely engender incommensurable classification systems.

To illustrate this thesis, consider a case where you are interested in discovering generalizations about the conditions under which people keep or fail to keep their promises. To develop this generalization, you need to identify situations of promise making, but it is highly unlikely that all instances of promise making will share physical characteristics that will enable them to be classified together in physical terms. The reason is that in different contexts we make promises in radically different ways (e.g., by shaking hands or saying "I promise"), but you'll still want to classify these situations together in developing a theory of promise keeping. Fodor also claims that this result is not a simple anomaly, but something we should expect if we consider the purpose of higher level theorizing. Higher level sciences are developed because we want to discover and understand relationships in nature that are not simply relationships between entities as defined in the lower level sciences. Different regularities appear salient at different levels in nature (see Wimsatt, 1976a, for further development of this claim). It is our interest in these regularities that directs how we develop our classification of events and we need to employ terms so as to capture these relationships without regard to how those events are classified at lower levels. This applies especially to psychology, which has different reasons for classifying events from those employed in neuroscience.

Further, Fodor (1978) claims that psychology would be impoverished if we insisted on equating psychological terms with neural terms. Part of the task of psychology, as Fodor views it, is to explain rational human action. This requires that we be able to describe the psychological state of a person in terms of an attitude (e.g., belief) toward a proposition ("Atlanta is in Mississippi"; for further discussion of such "propositional attitudes" in psychology, see Bechtel, in press a). The internal structure of the proposition is often critical to our psychological explanations. If a person believes that Atlanta is in Mississippi and also desires never to go to Mississippi, we can explain why the person never wanted to go to Atlanta. The person made an inference that we can represent in systems of formal logic. If we limited ourselves to the neural states that underlie these two mental states (the belief and the desire), the logical relationship between these propositions, which is critical to our psychological explanation, would be lost. All we would have is the causal relation between the two neurophysiological states. With only the neural information, we could not assess whether a person was rational. We would not be able to distinguish the previous person, who reasoned properly from false information, from another person who reasoned illogically from true information (e.g., the person who believes Atlanta is in Georgia and desires never to go to Mississippi and decides on that basis never to go to Atlanta). Hence, if we only had neuroscience theory we could not judge rationality and we would have lost explanatory power.[2] In some respects, then, the neuroscience theory is weaker than the psychological theory and so Fodor contends that we should not try to reduce the psychological theory to a neuroscience one. (For similar arguments that have been made in biology regarding the possibility of reducing Mendelian genetics to molecular genetics, see Hull, 1974, and Rosenberg, 1985.)

The development of bridge laws, which often seems to be an unproblematic requirement of the Theory Reduction Model, may pose serious difficulties. Some philosophers have drawn the conclusion that, due to the difficulties in constructing adequate bridge laws, higher level sciences, such as psychology, may not be reducible to the corresponding lower level science (e.g., neuroscience). Fodor, for example, draws the even stronger conclusion that higher level sciences are, in a strong sense, autonomous from the lower level sciences so that research in a higher level science like psychology must develop independently of work in lower level sciences like neuroscience. Moreover, because the two disciplines classify objects in their domains quite differently, lower level and higher level sciences cannot offer any useful guidance to each other, but must simply pursue their own problems in their own way.

The strong autonomy conclusion seems quite problematic, both on prin-

---

[2] Fodor acknowledges that if the neurophysiological state has the same kind of internal structure as the representation, this loss of information would not arise. But to require identifying such structure at the neural level would, he contends, imposes an additional requirement on reduction between cognitive science and neuroscience that would distinguish this case of reduction from other cases of scientific reduction. In normal cases of reduction, he contends, the lower level theory is developed without regard to higher level considerations and then the logical derivation is developed. In the following section I raise some doubts about this claim.

cipled and practical grounds. One principled ground is that the Theory Reduction Model does not require the kind of one-to-one mapping of higher level terms onto lower level terms against which the criticisms have been directed. Richardson (1979) argues that even Nagel, a major proponent of the Theory Reduction Model, allowed for multiple realizations of the same higher level property as long as one could explain why the different lower level states realize the same higher level state:

> Reduction demands only that there be a functional relation between the physiological and psychological domains: each physiological type, within specified boundary conditions, should map onto a psychological type. The "suitable relations" demanded by the conditions of connectability [in Nagel's account] need not be biconditional. Derivability, with its explanatory parsimony, is adequately accounted for, in turn, if only we find sufficient conditions at a lower level of organization capable of accounting for phenomena initially dealt with at a higher level; and this requires no more than a mapping *from* lower *to* higher level types and *not* a mapping from higher to lower level types. (p. 548)[3]

Patricia Churchland (1986, also Paul Churchland, 1984; Enc, 1983) appeals to the case of thermodynamics to show that a higher level property, temperature, is not always realized in the same way (in gas it is mean kinetic energy, but not in plasma or in solids) and yet thermodynamics is taken to be reduced to more basic physics. The reduction is accomplished by treating each reduction as domain relative. Churchland argues that domain relative reductions of psychological laws to neuroscience laws will be equally acceptable: "if human brains and electronic brains both enjoy a certain type of cognitive organization, we may get two distinct, domain–relative reductions" (Churchland, 1986, p. 357).

In addition to this principled objection to the strong autonomy position, there is also a pragmatic objection. Those who construe psychology as totally autonomous from neuroscience render it unable to benefit from research in neuroscience (and, presumably, unable to provide any guidance for work in neuroscience). Similar autonomy claims have been made previously in other sciences and the historical evidence suggests that insistence on such autonomy has been harmful to those disciplines.

---

[3] Richardson also contends that the fact that the same lower level state could realize different higher level states does not block theory reduction. The reductionist does not hold that lower level processes identified in isolation would always instantiate the same higher level property, but only when they are embedded in the same context. Critics of reduction (Putnam, 1978) argue that the whole context cannot in practice be invoked in such a manner as to permit the reduction. Although this may tell against the usefulness of theory reduction as a general strategy for integrating work in different disciplines, Richardson argues that it does not demonstrate the principled objection against reduction that Putnam and Fodor have maintained.

One example of the kind of error that results from maintaining such strong autonomy is found in physiological chemistry. In the 1840s physiologists confronted a task that was analogous in many respects to the task faced by contemporary researchers in cognitive psychology. They wanted to determine the processes by which animals utilize their food inputs in order to create heat and mechanical energy. Liebig (1842), one of the major contributors to the early development of organic chemistry, set out to devise an account of this process on the basis of his knowledge of the composition of the food inputs and the waste outputs of organisms. He also endorsed a strong autonomy principle, denying that it was necessary to carry out investigations on the actual intermediate processes occurring in the organism. He claimed that from the external data alone he could determine the processes that had to be going on inside the organism. Study of the internal mechanisms could only serve to fill in details of his model but could not show it to be wrong. Thus, like Fodor, Liebig postulated internal processes but denied the need to examine the physical mechanisms through which they were performed. In his model of animal metabolism, Liebig distinguished sharply between the functions of proteins and those of fats and carbohydrates. Because muscular structure is largely proteinous, he proposed that proteins were simply absorbed into the bodily structures and then broken down in the course of muscular work. Fats and carbohydrates, on the other hand, were consumed to maintain bodily heat.

Liebig's model was elegant, but seriously flawed. Liebig made a critical assumption—that the reactions in the body are all decompositional or catabolic, never synthetic. A priori, this assumption is quite plausible, but it is wrong. Moreover, it was only shown to be wrong when Claude Bernard carried out the kinds of chemical studies Liebig took to be unnecessary. Through his investigations, Bernard discovered that synthetic reactions are common in the animal body. Organisms break down some materials and rebuild others from these. Accordingly, dietary proteins are metabolized to amino acids and new proteins are synthesized to produce animal tissues. The energy produced from the breakdown of proteins is treated no differently than that produced from fats or carbohydrates. Such patterns of catabolic and synthetic reactions make perfect sense when one considers the need to maintain homeostasis in the body, but the important point is that the concept of homeostatic processes only emerged after Bernard discovered the occurrence of synthetic processes. They were not envisioned by those simply seeking to account for input–output relations. The insistence on autonomy for physiological chemistry thus gave rise to a model of nutritional processes that was grounded on an erroneous assumption. (I have discussed this and other cases in Bechtel, 1982.)

Another researcher who limited his focus to one discipline and as a result failed to utilize information from other disciplines that could provide useful guidance was Gall (1809/1835), the founder of phrenology. Although Gall is often belittled as nonscientific as a result of the quackery perpetuated by phrenologists (namely, the practice of trying to predict personality traits on the basis of the shape of people's skulls), his basic research strategy is a commonly accepted one. His first step was to identify psychological faculties that are responsible for different behavioral traits. He also sought to identify these psychological faculties with specific regions of the brain, theorizing that a person would exhibit the trait to the degree that the appropriate region in the brain was developed. The use of cranial protrusions was simply Gall's way of detecting the development of particular brain regions, based on the incorrect assumption that the cranium directly reflected the underlying brain structure. The critical part of Gall's program is simply to establish that there are specific faculties responsible for behavioral traits. Fodor (1983), interestingly, aligns his own program for psychology with that of Gall, for he too is interested in identifying faculties (modules) that are responsible for different kinds of information processing. Fodor's comparison of himself with Gall is apt, but it also reveals the weakness of pursuing the very kind of program Fodor advocates—one that develops the account of the mind independently of investigations at other levels.

One apparent difference between Gall's program and Fodor's is that Gall seemed to be interested in the question of where in the brain the faculties were located and thus seemed to integrate his psychological and neuroscience investigations. Despite this appearance, Gall too maintained a kind of autonomy for psychological inquiry, which is revealed in the way he developed his proposals and dealt with objections. Gall developed his account of different faculties simply by analyzing dimensions on which human behavior varies. He then treated each dimension as corresponding to a faculty and attributed individual differences to differences in the development of these faculties. What this step in Gall's program amounts to is positing modular subsystems for each trait (for a discussion of a more sophisticated version of this strategy, see Kauffman, 1971). Gall then attempted to correlate faculty development with brain development, but this step in his research did not influence how he identified faculties. This is revealed by the manner in which he responded to evidence derived from neurophysiological investigations. Flourens (1824) attempted to lesion areas to which Gall assigned particular functions in order to show that the resulting deficits did not correlate with deficits in the faculty Gall had assigned to the region. In particular, animals could retain functions when appropriate centers were destroyed. Gall dismissed this evidence, and yet it was the kind of evidence that could most effectively show where his analysis of faculties went astray. It was the kind of evidence that could undercut the assumption that character traits were due to the discrete mental faculties that Gall had posited. The pattern of deficits produced by brain lesions could show, for example, that character traits that were assigned to single functional units were really the result of cooperation of a variety of components and not the result of a single, localizable faculty.

Gall provides a particularly vivid example of the danger of cutting psychology off from evidence from neuroscience. Neuroscience research can at least show that the operations proposed in a particular psychological theory do not correlate with processes that are performed in the brain. This provides at least *prima facie* reason for looking for an alternative psychological theory that treats a different kind of function as basic. There are even further contributions that neuroscience might make. Information about the type of processes occurring in the brain when specific cognitive activity is being performed may suggest information processing models psychologists might usefully investigate. Thus, it seems plausible, if not likely, that information from neuroscience may be crucial in developing and evaluating psychological theories. To insist on the strong autonomy of psychology is to cut oneself off from such useful guidance and valuable information. Recognizing this, we need to consider further how psychological investigations might integrate with those of neuroscience.

REDUCTION AS FACILITATING
THE CO-EVOLUTION OF PSYCHOLOGY
AND NEUROSCIENCE

At the beginning of the previous section I indicated that one reason for opposing aspirations of reducing psychology to neuroscience was the fear that if reduction were achieved, psychology would be rendered redundant to neuroscience. Many reductionists argue, however, that this both neglects the contribution Theory Reduction can make in the process of developing a science and misrepresents what is actually accomplished in a Theory Reduction.

The fear that reducing one theory to another will make the reduced theory a mere application of the reducing theory neglects the critical role played by bridge laws and boundary conditions in carrying out a reduction. It is not an incidental matter to figure out how to apply a general theory to specific applications. A great deal of classical physics is only an application of basic Newtonian principles such as the law:

$$\text{force} = \text{mass} \times \text{acceleration}.$$

However, it took much research to determine how to apply this law to different circumstances. Moreover, when this law is applied to specific circumstances, it often yields results that were not anticipated by those who were already familiar with the general principle. Even if these are only special applications of the general theory, they are not, on that account, less interesting.

We could view the status of psychological theories, even if they were reduced to neuroscience theories, as much like that of the special applications of Newton's force law. The psychological theories would describe special consequences of the more general principles of neuroscience, consequences that only arise under special circumstances or background conditions. The laws of psychology will therefore supply additional information beyond that supplied by the neuroscience theories themselves, because they will specify the particular background conditions that apply in particular situations. Moreover, the current endeavors of psychologists in developing their theories will not have been wasted effort. The discovery of the higher level theories that will ultimately be reduced typically plays a major role in developing the reduction. Only in light of those higher level theories will it be possible to identify the background conditions that must be invoked in order to accomplish the reduction.

A more serious objection to invoking the Theory Reduction Model in the case of cognitive science and neuroscience is that the possibility of reducing cognitive theories to neuroscience theories seems rather remote at this point. One theory cannot be derived from another until there are precise, fully formulated theories in both disciplines. More recently, however, a number of philosophers have proposed a quite different role for the Theory Reduction Model. Wimsatt (1976a, 1976b, 1979) and Churchland (1986), among others, have proposed that developing reductions can play a role in theory development, not just in the *ex post facto* consolidation of already developed theories. Their idea is that if theory reduction is the ultimate goal, then we should use information from both the higher level and the lower level disciplines in the course of developing the theories themselves. If the theories co-evolve in this way, then, once the theories are developed, theory reduction will be readily achieved.

This co-evolutionary picture is supported by the fact that in most cases of reduction the theory that is reduced to a lower level theory is not the original upper level theory, but a revised form of that theory. Thus, it is not the original theory of phenomenological thermodynamics that is reduced to statistical mechanics, but a corrected version. Similarly, it is not Mendel's (or Morgan's) theory of genetics that is reduced to molecular genetics, but a revised version. To accommodate this feature, Schaffner (1967) developed a more general version of the Theory Reduction Model than that originally proposed by the Positivists. It views reduction as a two-step process. The first step is to derive from the lower level theory (together with bridge laws and boundary conditions) a corrected version of the upper level theory. The second step consists in showing that the revised upper level theory approximates the original upper level theory sufficiently well for us to see why the original upper level theory worked as well as it did (even though it failed in those cases where the theory constitutes an improvement). Although Schaffner did not discuss the possibility, it is of course possible that a new, lower level theory will be developed, as well, in which case we will need to show how the new lower level theory compares with its predecessor. Applying this expanded version of Schaffner's model to the case of psychology and neuroscience, the final objective is not to reduce current psychological theory to neuroscience theory, but to reduce a future psychological theory to a future neuroscience one (see Fig. 5.1).

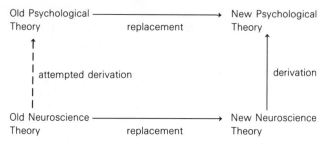

FIG. 5.1.   Complex reduction scheme including replacement of old psychological and neuroscience theories with new ones, and derivation of new psychological theory from new neuroscience one.

In Schaffner's own account, the two steps in a reduction are performed after the final theories are developed. The reduction enables us to see how the new, higher level theory and the old, lower level theory relate to one another. To create a co-evolutionary model (as in Fig. 5.1), it is necessary to modify Schaffner's model and construe the process of developing a new, higher level theory that coheres with the (potentially new) lower level theory as a step in the process of theory development. Moreover, we need to be aware that the use of the single term *reduction* may conflate two activities, one involving the relation of a higher level theory to a lower level one and one concerning the relation of a new theory to a predecessor (see Nickles, 1973; Wimsatt, 1976a, 1976b for other reasons for maintaining this distinction). Thus, we actually have a two-step process: the replacement of one higher level theory by another, where the relationship is between an old theory and its successor, and the interlevel reduction of the new psychological theory to a neuroscience theory. One reason to distinguish these steps is that the factors motivating the development of the new theory at a given level may have to do with developing an adequate account at that level as well as accommodating interlevel relations (see McCauley, 1986a).

The question that arises is: How are the two theories, one of which will ultimately be reduced to the other, to play a role in each other's development? Here Wimsatt (1976a, 1976b, 1979) argues for the importance of developing bridge laws that identify lower level and higher level processes (or the terms referring to those processes) at an early stage in the development of the theory. The goal at this stage is not to deduce higher level laws from lower level ones, but to identify points of disagreement between the claims made by the lower level and the higher level theories. For example, at the turn of the century, Boveri and Sutton developed evidence relating Mendelian genes with chromosomes, which previously had been identified simply as stainable structural bodies in the nucleus that seemed to play a role in cell division. They then focused on points at which claims made about Mendelian genes differed from those made about chromosomes. Given these differences, the information offered at each level suggested investigations at the other level. This resulted in revisions in the theories developed at each level. Here cross-level identification served as an hypothesis-generator, and so served a constructive role in theory development.[4] (A different perspective on the attempt to relate Mendelian factors to chromosomes is discussed in the next chapter.)

Advocates of reducing psychology to neuroscience, such as Patricia Churchland, foresee a similar process of integration advancing the development of these two disciplines. Each discipline can set the framework for investigation in the other, but can also profit by trying to accommodate the findings of the other. Thus, Churchland (1986) argues that "neuroscience needs psychology because it needs to know what the system does" (p. 373). The task for neuroscience is set in part by psychology just as the task for chromosomal genetics was set by Mendelian genetics—neuroscience theories are to account for psychological phenomena. A knowledge about how the underlying neural system works, however, may then lead to modifications in the psychological accounts of what the system is in fact doing. This will happen if it becomes apparent that the nervous system is not equipped to carry out the task as it was originally construed by psychology, but in fact performs a somewhat different task. To gain this new advantage, we must

---

[4] Hooker offers another example in which the attempt to develop the reduction served to guide the development of the theories at both levels involved:

> First, the mathematical development of statistical mechanics has been heavily influenced precisely by the attempt to construct a basis for the corresponding thermodynamical properties and laws. For example, it was the discrepancies between the Boltzmann entropy and thermodynamical entropy that led to the development of the Gibbs entropies, and the attempt to match mean statistical quantities to thermodynamical equilibrium values which led to the development of ergodic theory. Conversely, however, thermodynamics is itself undergoing a process of enrichment through the injection "back" into it of statistical mechanical constructs, e.g., the various entropies can be injected "back" into thermodynamics, the differences among them forming a basis for the solution of the Gibbs paradox. (Hooker, 1981, p. 49)

make a tentative mapping between the two theories, and then let the differences between them serve as guides for further research.

Churchland offers a number of reasons to expect a co-evolutionary research program between cognitive science and neuroscience to be successful. First, we assume that mental processes are in fact processes occurring in our brains and that both cognitive scientists and neuroscientists are investigating very related kinds of activity occurring in the mind–brain such as learning and memory. Second, in developing our ideas in any domain it is quite common to rely on models, and she contends that brains offer a better model for studying psychological phenomena than computers, which are commonly taken as a model by researchers in cognitive psychology.[5] She also contends that because our brains are the evolved product of the brains found in other organisms and because evolution is generally conservative, preserving successful designs already in use, work on other organisms with simpler brains may provide us useful models for understanding the information processing occurring in humans.

The opponents of reduction I discussed in the previous section posed a set of objections that they maintained undercut not only reduction of contemporary cognitive theories to neuroscience ones, but future theories as well. One objection claims that because the same psychological phenomenon could be realized in different substrates, including both human brains and animal brains, as well as computers and potentially the brains of aliens, it is impossible to equate a class of psychological phenomena with a class of neuroscience phenomena. Another objection contends that the classification scheme used for mental phenomena is employed for different purposes than that used to describe neurophysiological phenomena so that there is no point in trying to equate the two. In defending her co-evolutionary program, Churchland offers responses to both of these objections. To the first, she claims that we will simply need to carry out different reductions for each different kind of substrate in which psychological phenomena are realized. We may carry out different reductions of the theories about mental states of computers, aliens, humans, and other species but this, she contends, is no different than developing different accounts of temperature for gases, plasmas, and solids. Thermodynamics has accepted such bifurcation without detriment, so Churchland does not see the consequence as harmful to psychology.

With regard to the second objection, Churchland contends that the fact that psychological categories seem to be at cross-purposes to those of neuro-

---

[5] According to Churchland (1986):

> Brains are by far the classiest information processors available for study. In matters of adaptability, plasticity, appropriateness of response, motor control, and so forth, no program has even been devised that comes close to doing what brains can do—not event to what lowly rat brains can do. If we can figure out how brains do it, we might figure out how to get a computer to mimic how brains do it. (p. 362)

science is an artifact of the current level of theory development in neuroscience. At present, theorizing in neuroscience has been focused at very low levels, for example, at the level of single neurons. But increasingly neuroscience is looking at higher levels of organization and examining such things as the information processing and storage carried out by neuronal assemblies. Here, Churchland maintains, it is entirely reasonable to expect neuroscience to develop a conceptual apparatus which is compatible with the objectives of psychology. To support this claim she describes three such theoretical frameworks for higher level information processing by the nervous system that she suggests may provide a useful vehicle for connecting neuroscience concepts with those of psychology—Pellionisz and Llinas' (1982, 1985) tensor network theory, developed to account for the sensorimotor control achieved by the cerebellum, Crick's (1984) model of attentional processes, and connectionist or parallel distributed processing (PDP) models of perception (see McClelland & Rumelhart, 1986; Rumelhart & McClelland, 1986). The last example, although it constitutes a program being pursued primarily by researchers in artificial intelligence, is inspired in part by knowledge of some of the fundamental properties of the nervous system and the architecture of neural networks, and so represents the kind of cross-disciplinary bridge that could serve to unite neuroscience work and psychological work and facilitate the kind of reduction of psychology to neuroscience that Churchland recommends.

THE ELIMINATION OF FOLK PSYCHOLOGY IN FAVOR OF ONE THAT IS REDUCIBLE

Key to the co-evolutionary account discussed in the previous section was the idea that both psychology and neuroscience will need to change in the course of developing the reduction. One question that arises concerns how much change is tolerable before we have essentially dismissed the old theory and simply replaced it with a new one. In the revised model of Theory Reduction advanced by Schaffner and employed by Churchland the theory that was being reduced was supposed to approximate the old higher level theory, and so not totally displace it. There are, however, numerous cases in the history of science in which old scientific theories have simply been repudiated as false. In these cases advocates of the new theory typically do not bother to relate their new theory to the old theory because they do not recognize the old theory as even an approximation of the truth. In these cases we do not have a reduction of the old theory, but its elimination. A number of philosophers have maintained that such a fate will befall at least some of current psychology.

The claim that old theories get eliminated, rather than viewed as approximations to the replacement theory, is supported by Kuhn's analysis of scientific revolutions (see chapter 4). In describing these revolutions, Kuhn described new theories as incommensurable with their predecessors insofar as they use incompatible concepts to describe the world and make inconsistent claims about it. A commonly cited example of such a replacement was the replacement of the caloric theory of heat with the kinetic theory. Instead of heat being viewed as a fluid, heat came to be regarded as molecular motion. Those who accepted the new theory concluded that the term *caloric* simply did not refer to anything. Thus, there was no term in the new theory with which it could be equated. Other examples include the replacement of Ptolemaic astronomy with Copernican astronomy, of Aristotelian impetus physics with Newtonian momentum physics, of Newtonian physics with Einsteinian physics, of alchemy by chemistry.[6]

In the 1960s, a number of philosophers, including Feyerabend (1963b) and Rorty (1965), adopted the idea that a new theory may be incommensurable with an old one to argue that we should expect that current theories of mental states will themselves be replaced by theories of neuroscience. They contended that, once we developed adequate theories in neuroscience, we would take the same view of mental states as we now take of caloric or folk entities like demons. We would simply deny that they exist and would strike the terms referring to them from our scientific vocabulary. (For further discussion of this view, commonly referred to as *eliminative materialism*, see Bechtel, in press a.)

The case of psychology and neuroscience seems, in one critical respect, quite unlike the other cases of elimination previously noted and unlike cases of scientific revolutions. In those cases, the replacement theory was a theory of phenomena at the same level in nature as those it replaced. Neuroscience theories, however, will be at a different level (see McCauley, 1986a). If contemporary psychological theory is to be eliminated in favor of a new theory, it seems much more plausible that the replacement theory will have to be at the same level. Paul and Patricia Churchland, who, as we saw in the previous section, often argue for the co-evolution of psychological theory and neuroscience theory, also maintain such a modified version of the replace-

---

[6] Detailed analyses of these cases reveal some differences. In some cases it seems possible to show connections between the older theory and the replacement theory. For example, Tycho Brahe was able to show ways of mapping Copernican astronomy onto Ptolemaic astronomy and appealed to this account to show why Ptolemaic astronomy seemed to provide a good account of the observed movement of the planets even if its theoretical claims were not regarded as true. Sometimes the relationships could be made mathematically precise. For example, Newtonian physics can be shown to be a limiting case of Einsteinian relativistic physics in a variety of situations. In situations of low velocity the Einsteinian results closely approximate the Newtonian results. Similary, if one assumes an infinite maximal velocity, the Einsteinian equations give rise to the Newtonian ones. Even though one can make these comparisons, though, the point remains that in these cases, the new theory in inconsistent with the old and replaces it.

ment thesis. That is, while they envisage a co-evolutionary process occurring between cognitive science and neuroscience, they also expect that much of current psychology, especially what is commonly referred to as *folk psychology*, will simply be eliminated, replaced by a new cognitive psychology that is reducible to neuroscience.

The term *folk psychology* refers to our ordinary characterization of people in terms of their beliefs, desires, hopes, doubts, and so on. In ordinary life we not only use such expressions as "Cathy doubts that Jim will complete his Ph.D. this year" to describe a person's mental state, but we also use such expressions to explain and predict what people will do. Thus, we might explain why Cathy would not consider Jim for a faculty position in terms of her belief. Psychological discourse of this sort, the Churchlands maintain, is likely to be replaced by a new form of psychological discourse, one that adheres better with the kinds of theories that are developing in neuroscience. Although they cannot now offer detailed examples of what such discourse will look like, the idea is that it will invoke concepts of information processing more attuned to what the brain does than concepts like "belief" and "desire."

The Churchlands' case for the elimination of folk psychology is two-pronged. First, to make replacement seem plausible they try to establish the similarities between folk psychology and other folk theories which have been dismissed from our science. Second, they try to show why the framework of folk psychology is a dubious basis for a sound psychology.

To make the argument by analogy, they first must show that folk psychology is in fact a theory, since many people regard folk-psychological accounts, at least of themselves, as observational reports. The claim "I believe it is raining" seems simply to be a report of my current state and not grounded in a theory. Following Sellars (1963), however, the Churchlands maintain that our characterization of people including ourselves in terms of beliefs, desires, and so forth, is in fact based on a theory (Churchland, 1979). One way to recognize the theoretical character of such ascriptions is to recognize the interdependency of various ascriptions. When we ascribe a particular belief to ourselves or others we form expectations about a variety of other ascriptions. If these turn out to be false, we may retract our original belief ascription. A second way to recognize the theoretical character of folk ascriptions is provided by recent work in social psychology that suggests that people often confabulate about their own mental states, attributing to themselves reasons for action that could not be their reasons for performing the action (Nisbett & Wilson, 1977). This suggests that although we think we are merely reporting on our internal states, we may in fact be theorizing about them.

If folk psychology is a theory, the question of its truth arises. Here the Churchlands draw our attention to the fate of other folk theories, such as those of folk physics. These were once taken to be true, but are now rejected as false. Aristotle's theory of motion is such a theory. It is also one that captures the intuitions of most people even today who have not received specific training in physics. (See McCloskey, 1983, for a discussion of how contemporary, untutored students have ideas that accord more closely with these earlier scientific accounts than with contemporary science.) According to Aristotelian theory, an object will continue to move only so long as it continues to be pushed. Although it was recognized that some objects do continue to move after the external push ceases (e.g., a ball will continue in the direction it is thrown), it was thought that this was because a certain force, an impetus, was attached to the object. Once this force was extinguished, the object would stop travelling in the direction in which it was pushed. Thus, a ball will go as far as the impetus will take it, and then fall. Although the idea of impetus played a central role in Aristotelian physics and retains a place in the folk physics held by some people today, there is no such thing as impetus. An object set in motion will remain in motion unless acted on by another force. In the previous example, the other forces that act on a projectile and stop its flight are air resistance and gravity. The long acceptance of the concept of impetus, and its current acceptance by those who have not learned modern physics, does nothing to make the impetus theory true. The Churchlands argue that the long acceptance of folk-psychological states like beliefs and desires does not make folk psychology true. It may well go the way of folk physics.

The fact that other folk theories have proven erroneous does not itself establish that folk psychology is in for a similar fate. It might be the exception. The Churchlands contend, however, that there are serious faults with folk psychology that show the need to eliminate it. The main fault concerns the role folk psychology assigns to sentences or propositions. Beliefs, desires, fears, and so on, are standardly represented as being about sentences or propositions that state their content. Thus, one may have the propositional attitude of believing that Atlanta is in Georgia. The sentence "Atlanta is in Georgia" specifies the content of one's belief. The role of sentences in folk psychology, moreover, is not incidental. We compare the psychological states of different people in terms of whether they believe the same sentence or proposition. Moreover, we represent the reasoning of people in terms of the logical inferences they make upon the sentences that specify the content of their mental states.

The Churchlands maintain that this allegiance to sentences or propositions is quite problematic, especially when we consider how cognitive operations are performed in the brain. There seems to be nothing in the framework of neuroscience that plays the role of sentences. Moreover, the assumption that cognition involves logical inferences performed on sentences creates a dilemma: Do nonlanguage-using organisms or pre-linguistic human infants represent the contents of their mental states in sentences? Neither an affirmative nor a negative answer seems acceptable. If language users use sentences but nonlanguage users or human infants do not, then we have introduced a quantum leap in the evolutionary and developmental processes, and we cannot treat human cognition as a development upon earlier cognitive forms. If nonlanguage users or infants are thought to use sentences (perhaps in a language of thought as proposed by Fodor, 1975), then it is quite mysterious how they acquired their language (Churchland, 1980).[7] Given this and other difficulties, the Churchlands maintain that folk psychology, and any information processing psychology built in its mode, are likely to be erroneous and candidates for being replaced. Having appealed to neuroscience to repudiate folk psychology, it is not surprising that they also appeal to it for guidance in developing a new psychology:

> This "bottom-up" approach [deriving psychology from neuroscience] is not the only approach we might follow but it does boast a number of advantages: it is very strongly empirical; it is not constrained by the preconceptions of folk psychology; it has the capacity to force surprises on us; it permits a non-behavioral comparison of cognitive differences across species; it enjoys direct connections with evolutionary ethology; and at least in principle it *can* reveal the functional organization we are looking for. (Churchland & Churchland, 1981, p. 143)

The view that neuroscience will itself direct the development of a new psychology strikes many as implausible. In fact the Churchlands allow, as we saw in the previous section, that psychology, even an erroneous psychology, is needed to provide the behavior descriptions of what the neuroscience accounts are supposed to explain. Their contention is simply that neuroscience will show a way to supplant current psychology. Many philosophers, however, are dubious that neuroscience could ever force us to completely forego the categories of folk psychology. Our basic psychological notions are deeply seated not only in ordinary usage but in the theoretical frameworks of the social sciences. Moreover, they figure directly in our own attempts to provide norms for our scientific inquiry (see Horgan, 1987; McCauley, 1987a; Putnam, 1983). There is also another important difference many people see between the status of folk psychology and that of folk physics. Folk physics does not provide our understanding of what mechanics is about—it is simply one attempt to explain mechanical phenomena that has now failed. The concepts of folk psychology, on the other hand, seem to characterize in a crucial way what cognition is. Without using the perspective of folk psychology, it is not even clear that we can say what it is that cognitive science is supposed to explain.

There is an important distinction that can perhaps clarify this issue.

---

[7] For more on this problem, see Bechtel, in press a, chapter 4.

Although it is true that folk-psychological idioms have figured in the development of theories in modern cognitive psychology (see Dennett, 1981; Palmer & Kimchi, 1986), folk-psychological descriptions are most commonly used to describe people, not their internal operations. As they are used in the social sciences, the folk theories are not necessarily viewed as theories of internal processing but as descriptions of what certain systems know about their environment and how they are prepared to behave in it. This role may remain important even if psychology discovers that the internal processing activities themselves are not appropriately described in sentence processing terms and so repudiates cognitive theories that have employed explanatory tools taken over from folk psychology (Bechtel, 1985a, in press b).

The question of whether folk psychology will survive, or will be replaced in the wake of further research, is one on which people can only place their bets. Although some may think it will be impossible for humans to get along without folk psychology, the Churchlands are quick to remind us that folk theories do change and frameworks that seemed entirely natural in one era have been rejected as totally mistaken in another. We cannot exclude the possibility of even drastic revision in our contemporary folk and scientific psychologies. However, granting the revisability of psychological theory does not itself lead to the Churchlands' position. One can still question what criteria should direct the revision of contemporary psychology. The Churchlands appeal to neuroscience, but others might reasonably contend that neuroscience theory ought to be responsive to psychological theory and argue for neuroscience to obtain direction from the contours of psychological theorizing (McCauley, 1986a).

The concern with elimination is a by-product of attempting to understand the implications of reduction for psychology. What the issue of elimination adds to the discussion of theory reduction is the prospect of disposing of theories that do not fit the reductionist program (as either the reduced or reducing theory). This may be necessary if one insists on using theory reduction to relate cognitive science to neuroscience. Those who oppose the program of reducing psychology to neuroscience (either those like Fodor who maintain a principled autonomy for psychology, or those who reject the Theory Reduction Model as an appropriate model for integrating disciplines), of course, need not eliminate a theory in one discipline if reduction proves impossible.

IMPLICATIONS OF THE THEORY REDUCTION
MODEL FOR RELATING PSYCHOLOGY
AND NEUROSCIENCE

In this chapter I focused on the Theory Reduction Model as one model for relating disciplines and considered how it deals with the relation of cognitive science and neuroscience. The model, as I showed in the second section, is part of the legacy of logical positivism. If you accept the appropriateness of this model for characterizing relations between disciplines, two basic options are available. You can maintain that the model does not and should not apply to the relations between cognitive psychology and neuroscience, and then argue for the principled autonomy of psychology, and cognitive science generally, from neuroscience. Or you can claim that the model should apply and maintain that if it does not, then at least it offers a goal toward which the disciplines should progress through a co-evolutionary research program. I explored these options in the third and fourth sections. Finally, I explored the question of what happens if you accept the Theory Reduction Model and it turns out that current theories are not reducible. Here, the only option you have is to eliminate one of the current theories in favor of a replacement theory that is reducible. As I showed in the last section, typically those who adopt this option argue for eliminating folk psychological theories and creating new psychological theories that are reducible to theories of neuroscience.

One critical assumption that is made by the Theory Reduction Model is that the theories at all levels of science are basically used for the same purpose—explaining and predicting events in nature—and therefore should be completely commensurate with one another. The advocates of the principled autonomy of psychology maintain that the kinds of predictions and explanations that psychology is interested in may be different from those of neuroscience. The autonomy position, however, had the consequence that psychology and neuroscience were unable to inform each other. The problem is that it is difficult to make sense of different disciplines having different objectives and yet contributing to each others' objectives when the only tool for integrating disciplines is the Theory Reduction Model. That model treats all theories as simply concerned with explanation and prediction of phenomena in nature and construes upper level theories as simply special applications of more basic lower level theories. In the next chapter I consider an alternative model for integrating scientific disciplines that may offer greater potential for recognizing different explanatory and predictive objectives of different disciplines and yet allow for researchers in each discipline to draw upon contributions in other disciplines.

6

An Alternative Model
for Integrating Disciplines

INTRODUCTION: THE DESIRE
FOR AN ALTERNATIVE MODEL

In the last chapter I discussed the Theory Reduction Model as a vehicle for relating work in different disciplines and examined a variety of views as to the applicability of this model for relating cognitive science and neuroscience. As I noted at the beginning of that chapter, however, there is growing dissatisfaction with the Theory Reduction Model. I examine some of the objections to the Theory Reduction Model in the following section. In the remainder of this chapter I explore an alternative to the Theory Reduction Model, an alternative that will enable us not just to consider relations between cognitive science and neuroscience but also relations between disciplines within cognitive science.

SHORTCOMINGS OF THE THEORY
REDUCTION MODEL

Many of the objections to the Theory Reduction Model focus on the requirement that the laws of the reduced theory be derived from the laws of the reducing theory. It is not obvious that the necessary derivation will always be possible even when we possess fully developed theories at both levels. It may be that the information that is included in the lower level laws will be insufficient for us to derive the upper level laws. In Causey's (1977) account, the lower level laws will include that information about the components of the higher level entities that can be learned by studying them in isolation.[1] The higher level laws will characterize how these parts behave when included in higher level structures. The task of the reduction will be to derive statements about how these entities will behave when they become parts of higher level structures from the information about how these parts behave when they are independent plus information about how they are being combined into higher level structures.

It will not always be true that the properties we discover by studying the lower level entities in isolation will be the ones that are critical to explaining their performance in a complex system. For example, in studying a transistor taken out of a radio we may not attend to those of its properties that enable it to serve its function in the radio. Similarly, although studying the properties of amino acids in isolation may reveal their primary bonding properties, it may not reveal to us those binding properties that give rise to secondary and tertiary structure when the amino acids are incorporated into protein molecules. A similar situation may arise with neural structures. Researchers may only become aware of those properties of neural systems that permit them to perform cognitive tasks when they study systems while they are engaged in actual cognitive operations, not when they study them in isolation. This, moreover, is not just a hypothetical worry. Often, researchers who have taken systems apart and studied the parts in isolation have later discovered that they have failed to identify those properties of the components that enable them to play their role in the normal system.

One way around this difficulty is for researchers developing the lower level theory to incorporate into that theory those properties of entities that are revealed when the entities are incorporated into higher level structures. This raises the question as to how much we should be permitted to modify the lower level theory so as to facilitate the derivation of the higher level theory from it. Causey is reluctant to permit modification because unlimited revision of the lower level theory could trivialize the problem of reduction. We could simply incorporate all the information developed in the higher level theory as additional laws in the lower level theory.

Moreover, modifying the lower level laws to facilitate reduction may not serve the goal of unifying science, a major goal of the Theory Reduction Model. If the laws that need to be added to the lower level science to permit the derivation of higher level laws do not integrate well with those already developed at the lower level, no unification will be achieved. For example,

---

[1] In actuality, we are not studying them in total isolation from anything else, since we are studying them in the environment of the laboratory. What we are doing is studying them in isolation from their normal context within the system.

if the properties that enable amino acids to form secondary and tertiary structure are different from those that induce primary bindings, then we have two
lower level accounts, not one. However, Causey has no specific proposals
as to how to limit the acceptable modifications (see Hooker, 1981, and
Churchland, 1986, for accounts of reduction that are far more tolerant of
modifying lower level theories to accommodate upper level phenomena).

There is a further problem with treating the Theory Reduction Model as
a vehicle for unifying science. Numerous people have argued that systems
that behave similarly may in fact have widely different internal composition
(see discussion of Fodor in the previous chapter). The Theory Reduction
Model, however, requires us to treat these cases separately. If two memory
systems were organized in the same way, but one was made out of silicon
and another out of neurons, we would have to reduce the higher level principles of memory to two different lower level accounts, one concerning silicon
systems and one concerning neural systems. This fails to unify science. Instead, it splinters it, for we will end up with different laws where, before
reduction, we could treat the cases according to one common higher level
law. Pylyshyn (1984) raises this as an objection against reducing psychological
principles to neuroscience, for he claims that psychological principles allow
us to state generalizations (e.g., that people will answer the telephone when
they hear it ring) that would be lost and replaced with a myriad of different
principles if we insisted on distinguishing cases in terms of their underlying
neural process.

So far I have challenged the claim that Theory Reduction would unify
science. Even if it did, however, there remains the question of whether a
unified science is an important goal. As noted in the previous chapter, defenders of theory reduction point to two benefits it offers: ontological simplification and unification, and increased explanatory power. The ontological
simplification and unification arises from the fact that after theoretical reduction scientists in the reduced field will not have to worry about the status
of the entities described by their laws. Such ontological worries, however,
seldom seem to be of great moment in the doing of science. Rather, most
scientists seem content with Quine's maxim that what we take to exist are
the values of our bound variables—the objects referred to by our theories.
There are times when noting ontological connections does aid a scientist. For
example, recognizing that genes were units on chromosomes enabled researchers to investigate the nature and identity of genes more effectively.
Similarly, learning how cognitive processes are accomplished by the brain
may increase our understanding of cognitive processes. These benefits,
however, are not ones of ontological simplicity and, as I discuss later, can
be purchased without the Theory Reduction Model.

The other goal of reductionistic research programs—gaining explanatory
power—is potentially more significant. This, however, depends on accepting

the view that scientific explanation involves deriving a statement describing what is to be explained from other statements. As we noted in chapter 3, however, the adequacy of this, the deductive–nomological model of explanation, has been seriously questioned in recent years. Moreover, scientists often develop what seem to be perfectly adequate explanations of phenomena by staying on one level and tracing the causal processes operating at that level. Reduction does not seem always to be needed. This is not to say that there are not sometimes very good reasons to go to another level in nature for explanation. Richardson (1980a) argues that one of Dennett's major insights is to show that scientists frequently turn to other levels when a system they are studying does not behave in the way predicted by the principles they thought applied to the system. These deviations call out for explanation and sometimes going to another level will provide the explanation. Sometimes pure curiosity will lead scientists to inquire about how a system's constitution enables it to behave as it does. As we also see later, however, these explanatory objectives can also be obtained without the Theory Reduction Model.

Given these limitations of the Theory Reduction Model as a model for relating work in different disciplines,[2] it is time to see if an alternative is available.

DARDEN AND MAULL'S CONCEPTION
OF INTERFIELD THEORIES

One of the clearest alternatives to the Theory Reduction Model is Darden and Maull's (1977; see also Maull, 1977) conception of an *interfield theory*. Interfield theories do not attempt to derive one theory form another but rather seek to identify relationships between phenomena studied by two different fields of inquiry. Darden and Maull's focus on fields of inquiry reflects a shift away from the Positivists' conception of science as simply a matter of justifying theories and relating them to one another logically. The notion of a field recognized the importance of problems and techniques for solving problems in directing scientific investigations. Darden and Maull (1977) define a field as:

> an area of science consisting of the following elements: a central problem, a domain consisting of items taken to be facts related to that problem, general explanatory factors and goals providing expectations as to how the problem is to be solved, techniques and methods, and, sometimes, but not always, concepts, laws, and theories which are related to the problem and which attempt to realize the explanatory goals. (p. 44)

---

[2] See McCauley (1981) for further detailed criticisms of the Theory Reduction Model.

For Darden and Maull, the motivation to develop an interfield theory arises when researchers recognize that the phenomena in which they are interested are connected to phenomena in other disciplines, and that to answer their questions they must draw the needed connections between the phenomena. Given that the goal of an interfield theory is simply to identify these relations, there is no need to derive a theory of one field from a theory of the other. Here is a major break from the Theory Reduction Model.

There are a variety of relations between phenomena in different fields that an interfield theory might identify. It might, for example, identify in one field the physical location of an entity or process discussed in another, frequently revealing a part–whole relation between the entities studied in the two fields. It may also identify an entity characterized physically in one field with the same entity characterized functionally in another, or it may locate in one field the cause of an effect recognized in the other field. Darden and Maull illustrate the idea of an interfield theory with a number of examples. One of these examples I discussed in the previous chapter from the perspective of the Theory Reduction Model and it is useful to see the different perspective that emerges when it is examined as a case of developing an interfield theory. The chromosomal theory of Mendelian heredity established links between cytological phenomena and genetic phenomena. By 1903, geneticists had recognized Mendelian factors as the units of heredity, but had not identified their physical location. Independently, cytologists had discovered chromosomes and had determined that they were involved in hereditary functions. They could not, however, show how they played this role. In this setting, Boveri (1903) and Sutton (1903), proposed that Mendelian factors were located on or in chromosomes. This hypothesis was not proposed to achieve ontological simplification but rather was an empirical claim about how two kinds of phenomena were related. By assuming this relationship was true, investigators made new predictions and were able to carry out new kinds of investigation of both Mendelian factors and chromosomes. The identification of Mendelian factors and chromosomes provided the foundation for the classical genetics program of the Morgan school, which developed a detailed map of the location of genes on chromosomes and provided an explanation of why some genes seem to be linked while others assort independently. (For another case where three fields were joined, see Darden, 1986.)

In the cases examined by Darden and Maull there were clear problems in one field that required the resources of another field to answer. In other cases, however, the linkage between the phenomena in the domains of different fields was discovered fortuitously. An example is the discovery that several B vitamins constitute the substrate out of which various respiratory coenzymes are synthesized. This connection was not obvious either to nutrition researchers or metabolism researchers, both of whom looked at food as material to be consumed to produce energy. It was not until after researchers in each field reconceptualized the phenomena they were studying that the connection could be established. Once it was made, however, it provided a useful guide for further research because now researchers could use what was known about B vitamins to support their research on intermediary metabolism, and vice versa (see Bechtel, 1984).

There are a couple features of Darden and Maull's notion of interfield theories that deserve special notice. They view interfield theories as evolving to serve actual explanatory ends of scientists. In particular, interfield theories are developed and accepted because they facilitate inquiry that was previously not possible. Thus, unlike the Theory Reduction Model which is an abstract philosophical model, the account of interfield theories is designed to describe theories actually produced by scientists. It may therefore offer a more useful tool for understanding cross-disciplinary inquiry. Another distinguishing product of interfield theories is that the end product is typically a theory that spans fields, not two theories related by a derivation relation. This reflects the fact that researchers commonly are not interested in showing how one theory can be derived from another but only in the connections between the phenomena in the two fields.

As I noted in the previous chapter, the framework of theory reduction was designed to account for relationships between levels in nature. Although it is not necessary that interfield theories cross levels, it is one possibility. The point of developing an interfield theory that connects phenomena at different levels in nature, however, is not to give a complete account for the phenomena at one level in terms of processes at a lower level, but to answer questions that cannot be answered at the initial level. Many questions will turn out to have answers at the initial level in terms of the causal processes operating at that level and will not require appeal to other levels. However, some questions will require going to other levels. Such an appeal will not always be to a lower level. For example, to explain why my genes are located where they are in the world requires us to consider characteristics of people and how they migrate as part of social systems, not merely processes of DNA synthesis and replication, Here we appeal to higher level processes to explain the fate of lower level entities (Campbell, 1974b, refers to this as "downward causation").

One circumstance where it is important to appeal to higher level processes is to explain phenomena that are goal oriented. The term *teleological* is often employed for goal-oriented phenomena, but teleology has had a bad reputation during the past three centuries, during which the emphasis has been on mechanistic explanation. Pointing to the goal that something serves seems to conflict with the aims of mechanistic science because goals are realized in the future, whereas mechanistic science tries to explain phenomena in terms of past events. However, it seems nearly impossible to describe biological and psychological phenomena without introducing the language of goals or functions. It seems both true and important to identify a goal or function of the liver, for example, as making sugar for the organism to use.

There is a way of handling teleological phenomena in a mechanistic science, but it involves recognizing processes at different levels of organization in nature and drawing appropriate relations between them. Goal-serving devices often can be shown to be products of selection processes—the goal-serving device is present in a current organism because its presence in a previous organism aided that organism's survival (Wimsatt, 1972; Wright, 1976). What is important in this situation is that selection is operating on a level higher than that of the goal-serving device. Selection chooses the organism, for example, which contains the liver. Machamer (1977) recognizes that this interlevel relationship that gives rise to teleological talk connects levels in a quite different manner than does theory reduction. In explaining teleological phenomena one does not derive an account of what happens at one level from an analysis of the other. Rather, one shows how phenomena at one level fit into and are affected by processes at a higher level. Thus, teleological phenomena can be explained by an interfield theory that shows how a phenomenon at one level is situated in a higher level context and is present because of what it contributes in that context (see Bechtel, 1985b).

One way to construe the claims advanced on behalf of an ecological approach to psychology (Gibson, 1979; Neisser, 1975) is as an appeal to recognize that cognitive capacities are themselves adaptations of organisms that fulfill needs of organisms. An ecological approach can be construed as a strategy for examining psychological activity in the context of the organism and the selection forces operating on it. An ecological approach would thus require the development of interfield theories that connect investigations of psychological processing with ecological accounts of how organisms are adapted to survive in certain environments.[3]

Having acknowledged that sometimes interfield theorizing may require researchers to integrate their theories with those at a higher level, I focus for the remainder of this chapter on how the interfield theory model would deal with relations between cognitive science and neuroscience, and with relationships between disciplines within cognitive science itself.

---

[3] Sometimes the ecological approach is construed as a competitor to the information processing approach. Gibson, for example, speaks of organisms picking up information, and repudiates any interest in how they might process it. Instead he contends that psychology should only focus on identifying the information available to the organism, not its internal processing. The interfield theory model, however, suggests that this exclusivity is unnecessary—the processing account and the ecological account are accounts in different fields, each of which might benefit from developing interfield connections between them (see Bechtel, 1985a; Glotzbach & Heft, 1982).

INTERFIELD THEORIES BETWEEN COGNITIVE
SCIENCE AND NEUROSCIENCE

The relationship between cognitive science and neuroscience looks quite different when examined front the perspective of developing interfield theories than when considered according to the Theory Reduction Model. We can see the relationship as part of an attempt to develop a particular type of interfield theory, a *mechanistic explanation*. It fits into a long endeavor to understand cognition by showing how it results from a particular type of machine. Researchers of any given period are limited in their ability to think of the mind as a machine by the variety of machines available to which an analogy might be drawn. In earlier eras the steam engine and the telephone switchboard provided the examples, whereas today it is the computer. Yet, the goal of mechanistic research has remained the same for several centuries—to understand cognition by showing how it could result from processes found in known machines.

One thing that has been true of human-made machines, at least until very recently, is that they behave in the manner they do as a result of having parts that perform subtasks to the task of the overall machine. When we encounter an unfamiliar machine and seek to explain how it works, we typically take it apart, see how the parts work, and then attempt to rebuild the machine out of different parts. Researchers who think of natural systems, such as the cognitive system, as machines try to do the same thing. They try to take them apart to determine their components, see how these components function, and then either synthesize new machines from artificial parts or otherwise show how the parts working together could produce the behavior of these systems. At one level, the parts of the human cognitive machine are neural structures, so the task of explaining how the machine works may take us into neuroscience. But it need not, at least initially, for we often can describe the parts in terms of what they do, not their neural composition. What often differentiates cognitive scientists from neuroscientists is simply whether they identify the parts of the system as performing component cognitive tasks or as neural structures. These different ways of characterizing the system are often committed to the use of different techniques studying the behavior of these components. Yet, the overall strategy for both cognitive science and neuroscience remains the same—to show how the components of the mind-brain and their interactions produce the behavior of interest. Insofar as they are connecting behavior with the mechanism that produces it, researchers are developing interlevel theories and, insofar as these levels are studied in different fields (e.g., cognitive science and neuroscience), the attempts to bring them together will result in interfield theories.

Although philosophers have had little to say in a systematic way about the process of developing the kinds of interfield theories involved in mechanistic explanations, this is a subject ripe for investigation. There are some prominent characteristics of mechanistic research endeavors that are particularly relevant to cognitive scientists. First of all, underlying most mechanistic research is an assumption about how nature is organized. Mechanistic researchers assume that nature is organized in what Simon (1980) calls a "nearly decomposable" fashion. That is, the parts of the system are construed as modules operating in a nearly autonomous manner. A given module receives its input from another and sends its output to others in turn, but carries out its own operation on the input before sending it out. The ability of each module to perform its task is due principally to its internal properties. An analogy can be made to an office or a factory, where each individual knows how to perform a specific task and carries out that task on appropriate occasions (either when the appropriate job comes into the office or factory, or when another worker in the office or factory calls upon that individual to perform his or her task). The assumption that the system under investigation is in fact designed in such a nearly decomposable fashion is fallible,[4] but until very recently we have had no models of how to build machines or to investigate natural systems that did not make this assumption.

In actual practice, researchers trying to develop mechanistic explanations confront a number of important decision points, some of which can be briefly described (for more detailed discussion, see Bechtel & Richardson, in preparation). The first decision is to identify a system in nature that is a *locus of control* for the phenomenon in question. In actuality, this often is a very controversial decision. The conflict between cognitivism and behaviorism is largely a conflict over whether the mind–brain can be treated as the locus of control for behavior (receiving only inputs from the environment and producing behavior as output), or whether control over behavior must be located in a broader system that includes the reinforcement from the environment. The decision as to what system is the locus of control is crucial because we cannot begin to take a system apart until we have at least roughly identified its boundaries. However, researchers in cognitive science typically settle on the mind–brain as the locus of control.[5]

---

[4] Simon offers a priori arguments for why systems should be designed this way, but these are suspect.

[5] Deciding that a system is the locus of control for a particular phenomenon does not mean that the system is not sensitive to external factors or that it can be effectively studied in isolation from its environment. There are a host of ways in which factors external to particular cells can affect the oxidation processes within the cell. Similarly, if we identify the mind–brain as the locus of memory function, we should not think that memory phenomena can be studied without concern for the surrounding environment. External cues may in fact play crucial roles in the operation of memory. This does not invalidate the claim that the locus of control over memory is internal in the sense that the critical causal mechanisms through which remembering is accomplished are found within the system. But it does mean that researchers must remain watch-

Explaining how a given system is a locus of control requires decomposing it and showing how the parts of the system give rise to the behavior. A common first strategy is to seek a single component in the system that itself performs the task for the system. This strategy, which Bechtel and Richardson (in preparation) refer to as "direct localization," is exemplified in the investigations of such noted researchers as Gall and Broca. Gall, as I discussed in the previous chapter, tried to explain differences in character traits between people by positing a set of faculties, each of which was responsible for one character trait. Differences in character were due to differences in the development of the relevant faculties. As well, Gall tried to identify these faculties with regions in the brain by correlating the exhibition of the traits associated with a faculty with protrusions on the skull (which he took to indicate the degree of development of the relevant brain part). Here Gall exemplifies the major strategy of direct localization research—correlating system activities with characteristics of a part of the system. Underlying Gall's research was a strong modularity assumption that a behavioral trait is due to a component in the system. Once this assumption is made, the research strategy is quite natural—one must seek correlational evidence to show what component is responsible for the trait. Making this assumption constitutes the second major decision determining the character of a mechanistic research program.

Although Gall often is condemned as a charlatan, the strategy of attempting to correlate activities of a system with characteristics of a component of the system is widespread. Broca (1861), for example, in developing his claim that a region on the left temporal lobe of the cerebral cortex is responsible for articulate speech, also relied on correlational evidence, although of a different kind—that between damage to an area and loss of function. Often this correlational technique is expanded into an experimental procedure by inducing lesions to show deficits. An alternative to lesion techniques are stimulatory procedures where a region that is taken to be the seat of a particular function is stimulated to see if that results in the performance of the function in question (Fitsch & Hitzig, 1870, used such techniques to establish the existence of motor centers in area 4 of Brodmann, 1909).

Both the lesion and the stimulation procedures principally depend on establishing simple correlations—correlation of lesion with deficit or of

---

ful for external factors that figure critically in the operation of the system. A useful parallel here is the use of in vitro experiments in biology. In assuming that one can study a particular system in vitro one assumes that the locus of control for the phenomenon in which one is interested is to be found within the system. That assumption may be correct, but that does not mean that any result obtained through an in vitro study will be informative as to how the system operates in vivo. One risks missing environmental factors that are critical to the normal functioning of the system and being misled by artifacts that result under the abnormal environment. This is one point of caution that is emphasized by those who have advocated greater "ecological validity" in cognitive research.

stimulation with performance. Although such techniques often have figured centrally in research neither technique is highly reliable. The correlation of a lesion with a deficit does not establish whether the locus in question is itself responsible for the performance of the function or whether it plays only an ancillary role.[6] Similarly, the correlation of stimulation with increased performance does not itself establish that the locus is where the function is performed, for stimulation of that region may only serve to initiate activity elsewhere.[7] Perhaps more significant, however, is the fact that direct localization, no matter how correct, does not itself provide a mechanistic explanation. A mechanistic explanation requires showing how a system is able to produce the function, and a direct localization does not even attempt that. It only identifies a responsible subsystem.

A mechanistic explanation of a function requires, minimally, what Richardson and I refer to as a "complex localization" of the function. This requires not just the assumption that the system is nearly decomposable, but that different components perform different subtasks. A complex localizationist explanation then requires two things—a functional decomposition of the overall task into component tasks and a demonstration that there are components that perform each of these tasks. To develop the decomposition the researcher must figure out how the overall task could result from performing a set of simpler tasks that could be performed by different components. In

---

[6] It is reasonable to accuse Broca of failing in this regard because, although he did discover a portion of the brain that is responsible for speech performance, subsequent researchers, beginning with Wernicke, have identified other regions that also figure in speech behavior. In Broca's case, he did discover a region of the brain important to the function. But as Gregory (1961) shows, it is possible to make even more serious errors of localizing a function in an area which is far removed from the function in question:

> Although the effects of a particular type of ablation may be specific and repeatable, it does not follow that the causal connection is simple, or even that the region affected would, if we knew more, be regarded as functionally important for the output—such as memory or speech—which is observed to be upset. It could be the case that some important part of the mechanism subserving the behavior is upset by the damage although it is at most indirectly related, and it is just this which makes the discovery of a fault in a complex machine so difficult. (p. 323)

Gregory provides an example of how we might go astray: we might remove a resistor from a radio, producing a hum. That might lead us to construe the function of the resistor to be to suppress the hum in the system (Gregory, 1968, p. 99).

[7] The interpretation of Fitsch and Hitzig's work, which employed the stimulation technique, turns out to be much more complex. Brodmann's area 4 has been found to contain both sensory and motor fibers and not to be a pure motor area. Moreover, actual control of motor behavior depends on collateral activity in many other brain regions. Another good example of how one can be mislead by stimulation studies is provided by research on reward centers of the brain. Olds (1965) proposed a reward center on the basis of research showing that stimulation of certain areas of the brain would cause rats to pursue an activity nearly endlessly. Subsequent research, however, has shown that stimulation of other areas produces the same effect, challenging the interpretation that this is due to finding a specific reward center. (See further Valenstein, 1973.)

philosophy of mind, such analyses of cognitive activities into component activities often are referred to as *homuncular analyses* because they postulate that inside the mind there are a bunch of little agents (homunculi), each of whom carries out a small task. Although it may seem question begging to assume intelligent agents in explaining how people behave intelligently, circularity is avoided by requiring at each step that the posited homunculi are less intelligent than the overall system and carry out simpler tasks (see Bechtel, in press a; Dennett, 1978; Lycan, 1981). The second requirement is an empirical demonstration that there are components in the system that perform the tasks specified in the homuncular analysis. Here researchers must use the same techniques as figured in direct localizations—techniques that correlate the behavior of the component with changes in the behavior of the system. Here again, the most prominent techniques are lesion or stimulation procedures. The difference in this case is that the changes in the overall behavior will not be simply blocking or promoting the overall behavior of the system, but various ways of distorting that behavior that cohere with predictions about how the behavior should be distorted drawn from the functional analysis.

There are a variety of ways such complex localizationist explanations have developed historically, but a couple of examples serve to illustrate some of the possibilities and the issues involved. One example comes from current work in cognitive neuroscience. O'Keefe and Nadel (1978) developed evidence for two kinds of spatial memory systems, one of which involved an objective map of the environment, whereas the other relied on sets of directions for going from one place to another. They also produced evidence from lesion studies that the capacity for objective maps was localized in the hippocampus. This constituted a direct localization of the mapping function, but O'Keefe and Nadel recognized the need to explain how the hippocampus could perform this function. To satisfy this need, they developed a decomposition of the hippocampus into different parts on morphological and neurophysiological grounds. They then developed an analysis of how the activities in the different parts of the hippocampus could account for the overall task being localized in the hippocampus, the capacity to process mental maps. The significant features of this case is that O'Keefe and Nadel started with a direct localization of function, then made the decision to go to a lower level to explain how this function was performed. They employed information about the neural activity in the hippocampus to help them develop the homuncular analysis of how the hippocampus performed this function.

In other cases researchers have made different decisions about how to develop complex localizations. Once cells were identified as the locus of control for biological oxidations in the late 19th century, researchers tried to figure out how they performed this function. In the case of one oxidative reaction, fermentation, researchers initially proposed a direct localization of this activity in one enzyme. Evidence quickly mounted showing that this was incorrect and that many enzymes were involved. So instead of going to a lower level and developing an explanation of how the enzyme performed fermentation, researchers decided to develop a homuncular analysis at the same level. In this case they could not rely on physical information about enzymes to guide their search because the only way to identify enzymes at the time was in terms of their functions in promoting specific reactions. So instead, researchers proposed possible sequences of reactions and then tried to produce evidence that the appropriate enzymes for each enzyme in the sequences existed. On the basis of such investigations Neuberg (see Neuberg & Kerb, 1913) developed a very plausible model of fermentation with quite impressive empirical support.

Two differences distinguish the case of research on fermentation, as described so far, from that on spatial memory. First, initial direct localization proved incorrect in the work on fermentation so the explanatory endeavor stayed on the same level and, second, the components were identified functionally, not structurally. However, in this case, there is yet a further step to the story. Continued research seeking to distinguish physical steps in the process revealed that the initial decomposition was far too simplistic. In particular, it separated the fermentation system from other systems with which it was integrally involved. Moreover, it missed the fact that the steps in the reaction often are tightly linked with other steps, producing a system that is not so decomposable, but rather highly integrated. The end result was that in the 1930s a new model of fermentation emerged that was far more complex than originally expected, but that still fit the conception of a mechanistic model (Bechtel, 1986b). Fermentation is now understood as resulting from a complex mechanistic system in which a variety of parts each contribute to the overall task, but are each dependent on others for their ability to perform their task.

As these brief sketches indicate, there are a variety important decisions researchers make that determine the way mechanistic explanations are developed. For our purposes what we need to concentrate on is the character of the product of such endeavors. The product is not a theory derivation, but an interfield theory. What researchers produce is an analysis of how a function is performed in terms of the parts within the system. Researchers do not try to derive one theory from another, but seek a demonstration of how certain kinds of operations at the lower level give rise to the higher level phenomenon. The higher level science is not subsumed into the lower level science because the phenomena studied at the higher level (e.g., spatial memory and fermentation) are products of lower level activity. The interfield theory shows how they are produced, and so connects two levels of theorizing.

Moreover, the process of developing such interfield theories across levels tends to play an important role in developing theories at each level. The division between two types of spatial memory systems, for example, guided

O'Keefe and Nadel's work, for it informed them as to what kind of memory to look for in the hippocampus. The information about the structure of the hippocampus, in turn, provided suggestions as to the types of processes involved in carrying out spatial memory tasks. Conversely, the search for enzymes in fermentation was guided by assumptions about the kinds of steps needed to perform fermentation. The emerging evidence about the physical substrate, however, was instrumental in revising initial assumptions about the nature of the system and guiding researchers to a new homuncular analysis of the process.

In the previous chapter, I described how those opposed to reducing psychology to neuroscience via the Theory Reduction Model have maintained that total autonomy of cognitive theories from neuroscience ones is the only alternative to reduction. The mechanistic interfield theories sketched here open another possibility. This model can accommodate interaction between cognitive and neural inquiries without requiring reduction. It allows both analyses to inform each other in the attempt to develop an interfield theory, but does not require subsuming one explanation under another. Von Eckardt (1978) provides a useful analogy. We might develop a functional analysis of how a particular omelet-making machine makes omelets. The steps in our analysis, however, may not correspond to those actually performed by the omelet maker. One way to find out that we have the wrong functional analysis would be to discover that there are no components within the system that perform the various tasks identified in our functional analysis. (See the discussion of Gall and Liebig in chapter 5 for similar cases from the history of science.) Merely rejecting a mistaken functional analysis, however, is not the only contribution. The attempt to identify components performing functions may provide further insight as to how to develop the functional analysis. Starting with what the parts do, we may be guided to a different conception of how the system actually operates.

Unlike the Theory Reduction Model, the model of an interfield theory does not require that the lower level give the final verdict. A further example from von Eckardt shows how the higher level might override lower level considerations. She criticizes an argument by Geschwind and Kaplan (1962) that a particular class of patients, commonly classed as *agnosics*, should be reclassified as only having a naming deficit. Geschwind and Kaplan had argued that positing an object recognition center was unnecessary and so maintained on grounds of simplicity that we should reclassify the two deficits as one. Von Eckardt argues both that the data do not count against the more classical model that posits an object recognition center and that an object recognition center should be accepted because the object recognition process figures centrally in other information-processing accounts in psychology. Positing such a center provides a better explanation of how ordinary people behave. Thus, the ability of the functional analysis to explain the overall functioning of the system becomes a consideration in evaluating the interpretation of a particular lesion result. (See Wilkes, 1978, 1981, for additional discussions of potential interactions between levels.)

Another fruitful case where functional considerations have led to reevaluation of claims made on the basis of neural investigations alone is found in recent reinterpretations of the contributions of Broca's and Wernicke's areas to language processing. The traditional interpretation held that Wernicke's area was a language comprehension center and that Broca's area was responsible for language production. This interpretation was grounded not only in the fact that lesions in Broca's area manifest themselves most clearly in speech production, whereas those in Wernicke's area serve to incapacitate comprehension, but also by the acceptance of an associationistic model in which inputs were processed in one channel until an associated output process was initiated. The categories of analysis in modern linguistics, however, do not emphasize the comprehension–production distinction of the aphasia researchers, but instead employ the categories of phonological syntactic, semantic, and pragmatic analysis. Researchers trained in modern linguistics therefore sought to reinterpret the aphasia data within the framework of linguistic theory.

When they carried out this reanalysis, these researchers found evidence that, contrary to the traditional interpretation, Broca's aphasics do manifest comprehension deficits. These arise when distinctive syntactic or syncategorimatic terms are critical to the sentence's meaning and where this meaning is not redundantly coded by the semantics of other terms. For example, in the sentence "Place the napkin on the plate" the word "on" is critical because it would be equally possible to instruct someone to place the napkin under the plate. On such sentences Broca's aphasics will manifest comprehension deficits. Upon further examination, these researchers were able to show that whereas normal subjects process syntactic indicator words (e.g., "on") far more rapidly than ordinary content words (e.g., "table"), Broca's aphasics were unable to do so (Bradley, Garrett, & Zurif, 1980). These researchers therefore proposed that Broca's area was responsible for syntactical analysis, not language production. Here a psycholinguistic perspective figured centrally in revising an account originally developed from more neurally based aphasia studies. More recent extensions of the research, however, seem to be pointing to possible revisions in the linguistic perspective itself. The proposal has been advanced that Broca's area may not be specifically involved in linguistic function, but may be more generally involved in automatic functions generally (Grodzinsky, Swinney, & Zurif, 1985). Such a proposal challenges the very idea of a modular speech processing unit that has been basic to both the aphasia tradition and the Chomskian tradition and suggests a closer integration of linguistic capacities with other cognitive capacities (for further discussion, see Richardson, 1986).

The process of developing mechanistic explanations through complex localization described here provides an alternative account of relations between levels in science to that offered by the Theory Reduction Model. But it is important to emphasize that it is built upon an assumption—that nature is designed in a decomposable, modular fashion. Although the mechanistic program has made major progress in the life sciences during the past three centuries, it has also been frequently criticized. Critics of mechanism in biology often have been called *vitalists*, whereas psychological opponents have been labeled *dualists*. These labels actually subsume a wide variety of different positions, but they all encountered a common problem. Without the decomposition assumption, no explanatory research program seems possible. A scientist might describe the behavior of a system but, without taking it apart, cannot explain why it does so. The only possible explanation is to ascribe the behavior to a vital power or an immaterial mind that manifests itself in the particular behavior.

Recently, however, an alternative perspective has arisen that does not require decomposing operations into component operations. Traditional cognitive models have decomposed cognitive tasks into rules for manipulating representations. This is not true of the recently proposed parallel distributed processing systems (PDP systems, also known as *connectionist systems*). These systems are built from very simple units. These units are connected to each other so that they can activate or inhibit each other. The system works by thermodynamic principles so that after an initial input, the units pass activations and inhibitions between each other until a stable state of minimal energy is realized. The pattern of activity supplied to the system as input represents the assignment of a task to the system while the resulting stable pattern represents the system's solution to the problem. The behavior of the system is determined totally by these local operations, particularly the connections between units, and so is not governed by rules that break the overall task into component tasks. Although the overall processing may more or less accord with certain cognitive rules, these rules do not figure in the operation of the system. The rule-like behavior is simply an emergent product (McClelland & Rumelhart, 1986; Rumelhart, 1984; Rumelhart & McClelland, 1986).

In PDP systems, the overall task is not the result of performing component tasks that are characterizable from the perspective of the overall cognitive task and so one cannot decompose the system into component cognitive operations in order to explain it. The operations within the system are of a quite different kind—passing of excitations and inhibitions between nodes. The behavior results not from special operations performed by components but from the character of the overall patterns of interactions of large numbers of very simple components. What researchers can do is show that the resulting system behaves appropriately so as to be characterized in cognitive terms without showing how the behavior arises step by step.

PDP systems, thus, violate the decompositional principle on which more traditional mechanistic systems are based and provide an alternative to these more traditional mechanistic accounts. If our cognitive system is a PDP type system, then the mechanistic research strategies outlined in this section may not work, because they would lead us to look for discrete components and not to focus on patterns of interaction. But this failure will not show that drawing connections between levels is misguided, but only that a different type of interfield theory will be required. This theory will show how PDP systems are able to produce behavior describable in cognitive terms. The strategies for developing these theories will be different, for understanding will not result from taking the system apart. Rather, it will result from understanding mathematical models that show that systems of certain kinds will behave in certain ways. But the result will still be an interfield theory showing how certain kinds of processes give rise to other process (Bechtel, 1986c).

INTERFIELD THEORIES
WITHIN COGNITIVE SCIENCE

In the previous section I have shown how the concept of an interfield theory gives a different perspective on the relationship between cognitive science and neuroscience, a relationship that has been of central interest to those attracted to the Theory Reduction Model. But there is another kind of interfield relationship that the Theory Reduction Model is not even designed to handle, that between disciplines within cognitive science (e.g., psychology, artificial intelligence, linguistics, anthropology, and philosophy). Because these disciplines deal with phenomena at roughly the same level of organization in nature, so that no part–whole relations obtain, it does not make sense to propose deriving theories in one of these disciplines from those in another. The only reduction relation that might obtain is if several of these theories were all subsumed under the same lower level theory. But yet it is clear that the creators of cognitive science envisioned the development of interesting theoretical relationships between the contributing disciplines without that sort of reduction. The notion of an interfield theory can be usefully applied in these contexts. For this analysis, I focus primarily on relations between psychology and linguistics.

In previous work (Bechtel, 1986a), I have introduced the term *cross-disciplinary research clusters* for areas such as cognitive science in which practitioners of different disciplines, recognizing that they were studying very related phenomena, have attempted to foster such integration of their work. In part, these cross-disciplinary research clusters are characterized by institutional arrangements—the development of joint conferences, of interdisciplinary journals, and of interdepartmental programs or centers in universities. These institutional structures are critical because they open channels for professional development that otherwise might be closed. Traditional disciplines are often "ethnocentric" (Campbell, 1969) due to the way reward systems are established in the disciplines. For example, departments are designed to train students in the central areas of the discipline and the most prestigious journals focus on the central issues in the discipline. The existence of cross-disciplinary journals, conferences, and university centers provides an alternative avenue for professional development as well as opportunities for practitioners of each discipline to learn from each other.

My particular interest here is in the character of the theorizing that can emerge in these cross-disciplinary research clusters. Abrahamsen (1987) has introduced a useful distinction between boundary-breaking and boundary-bridging contact between disciplines, each of which involve a different kind of theoretical endeavor. Boundary-breaking contact occurs when practitioners of one discipline turn to a different discipline for a new way of construing their own discipline, or when practitioners of one discipline seek to bring part of the territory of another discipline under their aegis. Boundary-bridging contact, on the other hand, occurs when practitioners of one discipline attempt to draw upon work in a related discipline to solve problems as these problems are defined within their own discipline. Abrahamsen tries to show that both kinds of endeavors have occurred and played an important role in the history of interaction between psychology and linguistics.

It is typically the instances of boundary breaking that receive the most attention. Blumenthal (1987) describes two major instances of boundary-breaking relationships between psychology and linguistics. Both occurred at a point when practitioners of one discipline found their theoretical resources impoverished and sought to expand them by incorporating a theoretical framework from another discipline into their own discipline. In the late 19th century it was linguists who were dissatisfied, and turned to the new psychological perspectives being advanced by investigators like Hobart and Wundt. Here they saw the hope of developing an approach to the study of language that was empirical and quantifiable. Part of their endeavor was to show how the tools for investigating mental processes in psychology could be invoked to account for the structure of language. Partly as a result of the diversity of views about cognitive processes within psychology and partly as a result of the rise of behaviorism, this cross-disciplinary endeavor came to an end early in this century. The period of exchange, though, left a legacy, in the form of structuralist linguistics, on linguistic studies long after the contact with psychology ended.

In the 1960s linguistics returned the favor by infusing a new perspective into psychology. Chomsky was in the process of reconceptualizing the task of linguistics, and in particular offered an alternative to the structuralist analysis of language with his model of generative grammar. During this period numerous psychologists like George Miller, Thomas Bever, and David McNeill found the theoretical framework of behavioristic psychology impoverished and saw in Chomskian linguistics a potentially useful framework for psychology. The transformations proposed in Chomsky's grammars suggested operations that might occur in the mind and, moreover, it seemed possible to seek data to confirm whether such transformations do occur (Miller, 1962).

Not only did modern cognitive psychology borrow from Chomsky at the outset, but Chomsky willingly construed his work as a contribution to psychology (Chomsky, 1968). On the basis of his linguistic analysis, Chomsky claimed to be able to draw psychological conclusions such as his nativistic conclusion that knowledge of grammar is innate, not learned. This claim was supported in part by linguistic evidence (the evidence for a Universal Grammar), but also on psychological grounds (the argument that the stimuli language learners receive are too impoverished to permit learning). Another contribution Chomsky tried to make to psychology was his distinction between competence and performance, which he saw as serving to allocate responsibilities for further inquiry between the two disciplines. Universal Grammar constrains the principles of grammar for natural languages and it is mastery of these principles that constitutes competence. Because Universal Grammar is both universal and innate, linguistics could develop, relying on its own resources, the theory of competence, leaving to psychological investigators the study of the limitations on actual language performance stemming from memory and processing capacities.

What occurred in these two boundary-breaking cases was the attempt to invoke (or impose) a theory of one discipline to restructure another. The two disciplines were not mutual partners in creating an interfield theory but rather an already developed theory in one discipline was simply extended to answer questions in the other field. Because the linguistic theory was now being called upon to answer different kinds of questions (e.g., questions about mental processing rather than the structure of language systems) than those for which it was designed, it is not surprising that further research called it into question. The result is that the initial attempts to integrate disciplines in this way failed. Consequently, interest in the cross-disciplinary program proposed by Chomsky has dwindled both within psychology and linguistics. As Reber (1987) and McCauley (1987b) try to show, this is partly due to the fact that different demands were put upon the theories in linguistics and psychology, and practitioners in each discipline addressed themselves primarily to the demands of their own discipline, and not to building an interfield theory.

The picture that emerges from looking at the exchange between psychology and linguistics as a boundary-bridging endeavor, however, looks quite different (see Abrahamsen, 1987). Here there is no attempt to make the theory of one discipline do the work of another, but rather to draw useful connections between the investigations in each discipline. Such connections may generate true interfield theories. To understand the interaction between psychology and linguistics as an interfield endeavor, we need to begin by recognizing that psychology and linguistics, while both studying features of language, construe language differently. For many linguists (but not Chomsky), language is primarily a cultural product that has an interesting structure that is to be analyzed abstractly. For psychologists, language is something that is comprehended and produced by organisms, and the interest is centered on investigating those real-time processes.

Different accounts of language may facilitate these two ends, yet these accounts may each be informative to those pursuing other ends. In order to develop a processing model of how organisms represent and manipulate language, psychologists need a description of language. Linguists' descriptions provide a useful starting place, but they may need to be reformulated to provide a processing account. The research of Clark and Clark (1977; a psychologist and linguist, respectively), illustrate how psychological inquiry may begin with descriptions of language drawn from linguistics, but then reformat these descriptions in the course of psychological investigations. They reformatted linguistic accounts of such phenomena as negation and comparatives into process ready formats that were then incorporated in processing models. They then used psychological data such as error patterns and response latencies to evaluate the psychological adequacy of the models.

This research and other cross-disciplinary endeavors by psychologists who appeal to linguistic analyses in the course of their work (Abrahamsen, in preparation; Gleitman & Gleitman, 1970; Kaplan & Bresnan, 1982; Klima & Bellugi, 1979) do not simply apply the theory of one domain to another, but reformulate a theoretical perspective or result from one field so as to guide research in another field. In the process, psychologists may specify connections between language processing and the abstract structure of language and so produce interfield theories that span the fields. These theories show how the mechanisms studied by psychology can give rise to the structures of language, viewed as a cultural product. In carrying out these investigations, however, psychologists neither attempt to supplant the endeavors of linguists nor advocate psychological hegemony.

The relationship between psychology and linguistics is not unidirectional and limited to psychologists borrowing linguists' descriptions and modifying them to guide their search for processing mechanism. Psychology can serve to explain linguistic phenomena by showing some of the underpinnings of language and limits on the kinds of languages that could be employed by humans. For example, psychological information about processing constraints may explain why certain types of linguistic structures predominate, such as the predominance of right-branching over left-branching or center-embedded structures (Yngve, 1960). Here the psychological investigation can explain phenomena described, but not explicable, within linguistics itself. Thus, both the psychological use of linguistic theory and the appeal to psychological explanations for linguistic phenomena result in theoretical developments that cross disciplinary boundaries. Features of the abstract structure of language are connected to features of the system that comprehends and produces language. (For more details, see Abrahamsen, 1987, from whom the previous account is drawn.)

Boundary-bridging relationships are where we would most expect to see the kinds of interfield theorizing that Darden and Maull describe, for here the emphasis is not on borrowing or imposing theories, but on drawing connections between phenomena studied in different disciplines with diffe :ent orientations. In these cases, researchers in each discipline can enrich their own understanding of the phenomena in which they are interested by discovering how these phenomena are related to other phenomena.

Examples of such cross-disciplinary theorizing also can be located in other areas of cognitive science. One project where practitioners from a variety of disciplines are now contributing to the development of a theoretical perspective that may eventual span these disciplines is an investigation of the nature of concepts and categorization.[8] (The idea of a concept is here taken as a linguistic or mental representation for a category of things.) The roots of this endeavor are often traced to the philosopher Wittgenstein (1953) who challenged the classical view that concepts could be defined by, for example, providing the necessary and sufficient conditions for being in the corresponding category. He maintained that even for a simple concept like "game" it is not possible to state necessary and sufficient conditions. He suggested that rather than there being a common set of properties shared by all games, there might be an overlapping set of properties, of which any given game might share some but not all. He compared the situation to that found among members of a human family, each of whom possess some of an overlapping set of traits, but where no one trait is shared by all and only members of the family.

The challenge to the traditional conception of concepts was further developed by Berlin and Kay (1969), two anthropologists interested in linguistic structures. Although it had been generally believed that different cultures simply classified colors differently, they showed that in different cultures with widely varying languages, if the culture had a word for a particular color, people took the same example of that color to be focal. The languages might differ in the range of color terms available, but not in what were taken to be focal colors.[9] This work was further developed by the psychologist Eleanor

---

[8] Some of this material was discussed from a quite different perspective at the end of chapter 2.

[9] Kay and McDaniel (1978) tried to provide a neurophysiological foundation for this result.

Rosch and her colleagues. Initially, Rosch showed that even in cultures where the languages did not have terms for basic colors, people still processed focal instances of those colors in a more basic fashion than nonfocal colors (Heider [Rosch], 1971, 1972).

Rosch then extended this idea beyond colors to a wide variety of concepts (e.g, "bird") and showed that they too possessed a similar structure, so that some instances of a category (e.g., a robin) would be judged more prototypical than others (e.g., a duck) (Rosch; 1975; Rosch & Mervis, 1975). In addition to linguistic evidence, Rosch and subsequent psychologists have developed a wide range of psychological measures (e.g., reaction time measures that show faster reaction times for categorizing more prototypical instances of a category) that help to further elucidate this account of the structure of concepts.

Rosch subsequently repudiated the idea that the evidence she had compiled showed that people actually made judgments as to whether an object belonged to a category on the basis of its similarity to a specific prototype or that concepts were mentally represented in the head in terms of prototypes (see Rosch, 1978). Numerous other psychologists, however, interpreted the results that way. Brooks (1978) and Medin and Schaffer (1978), for example, advocated an exemplar model of mental representations wherein an individual instance of a category (a dog one is familiar with) would serve as a reference point in categorization decisions and a person would judge whether another object was a member of the category in terms of its similarity to the exemplar. (See Smith & Medin, 1981, for a review of this research. See also Barsalou's volume in this series.)

This new approach to concepts and categorization in terms of prototypes attracted a variety of critics from the same diversity of disciplines. Two groups of psychologists, Osherson and Smith (1981) and Armstrong, Gleitman, and Gleitman (1983) have challenged the view that categories literally have a prototype structure, as some defenders of the prototype view have held. Armstrong et al., for example, show that prototype effects occur even with a concept like "odd number," which would seem to be a paradigmatic example of a concept with necessary and sufficient conditions. Osherson and Smith endorse a view, articulated previously by Miller and Johnson-Laird (1976) and by Smith, Shoben, and Rips (1974) that concepts have both a defining core (which stipulates necessary and sufficient conditions for category membership) and an identification procedure (which induces the prototypicality results). A philosopher, Georges Rey (1983), has also joined in criticizing the Roschian tradition, arguing that the correct understanding of linguistic meaning is a metaphysical matter that should be kept separated from facts of psychology. Following Putnam (1975b), he takes the core of meaning to consist in the reference relation through which words connect with the external world. Those objects referred to constitute the word's extension, and the extension of a term is an objective matter that is independent of how any individual determines what falls within the extension of a term. Thus, he rejects the claim that prototypicality judgments have any bearing on the meaning of language. (See Rey, 1985; Smith, Medin, & Rips, 1984, for continuing discussion.)

Others have joined in the criticism in different ways. A linguist, Anna Wierzbicka (1987) has taken seriously Wittgenstein's injunction to those defending the classical view (that concepts are defined in terms of necessary and sufficient conditions for category membership) not simply to assume that there are necessary and sufficient conditions governing category membership, but actually show what these conditions are. But unlike Wittgenstein and those who have adopted the prototype conception, she maintains that it is possible to provide necessary and sufficient conditions for concepts like "game" and offers candidate definitions. She does not, however, dismiss the prototype approach totally, for she argues that the definitions of some terms, like *red*, *bird*, and *climb*, do encode a comparative judgment in their necessary and sufficient conditions and so rely on prototypical instances in the definition itself. Two psychologists, Medin and Ortony (in press), drawing on a variety of these criticisms, advocate a psychological essentialism according to which representations of concepts do encode essences. However, Medin and Ortony take these essences to lie in rather deep theories, not in surface characteristics. They hold that these theories generate a more superficial set of features (e.g., visual features) that can be used for identification of instances of a category and that our visual system has evolved so as to be responsive to just such features. These, however, are not the defining characteristics.

A number of theorists supportive of the Roschian tradition (again drawn from a number of disciplines) have also begun to invoke deeper cognitive structures like theories to account for prototypicality judgments. The psychologist Neisser (1986) argues that although our ability to categorize may begin with the ability of the perceptual system to respond to patterns of organization in the world, it ultimately relies on theories for determining what belongs to a common category (see also Murphy & Medin, 1985). George Lakoff (1987), a linguist, has introduced the notion of "idealized cognitive models" to refer to the organizing units of knowledge that affect our categorization of objects. These models provide organizing principles for our thinking and it is these, Lakoff claims, that give rise to prototypicality judgments. One such organizing notion is that of metonymic models, which Lakoff developed in the course of a joint investigation of metaphor with a philosopher, Mark Johnson (Lakoff & Johnson, 1980). These are models in which a part of a category represents the whole category in such tasks as reasoning and recognition. An example would be letting one conception of a mother, the housewife mother, serve to represent the whole category. Once this happens, prototypicality judgments, such as the judgment that a working mother is a less good exemplar of a mother than a housewife, result. Another organizing principle involves radial categories that arise when, starting from a central case, we define a variety of variant cases. Using the example "mother" again, we can start with the central case of a mother who gives birth to the child, supplied half the child's genes, nurtured the child, and so on, and define special cases that deviate from this pattern (e.g., stepmother, adoptive mother, birth mother, etc). These models all deviate from our idealized model and this also, according to Lakoff, helps generate prototypicality judgments.[10] Lakoff proposes that concepts and categories are the product of these deeper cognitive models, and so are not simple atoms of thought.[11] (A generally favorable review of this conception of concepts and categorization is given by another philosopher, McCauley, 1986b.)

In this work on concepts and categorization, we find a number of researchers from different fields in cognitive science all addressing the same issue, the nature of our concepts. As a result of coming from different fields, however, they have brought different theoretical models and different modes of investigation to the work on concepts and categorization. Although there is considerable disagreement about the early results on prototypicality judgments, what researchers are working toward is an account of concepts and categorization that is adequate to the demands of the several different disciplines involved in cognitive science. Such an account would provide another example of an interfield theory that bridges disciplines without any sort of reduction of one discipline to another.

CONCLUSIONS CONCERNING
CROSS–DISCIPLINARY RESEARCH

In the previous chapter I addressed relationships between disciplines from the perspective of the Theory Reduction Model and showed a variety of views about the relationship of cognitive science and neuroscience advocated by people who have accepted this as the model for relating disciplines. In this chapter I began with criticisms of the Theory Reduction Model and then developed an alternative view of the relationship between disciplines based on Darden and Maull's notion of interfield theories. I tried to show that the

---

[10] Lakoff further argues that our cognitive models result in a very direct sense from the fact that we are embodied cognizers. Thus, he maintains that we cannot understand cognition by construing it formally as a symbol manipulation process but must understand it in relation to the kind of body we have and how we live in the world.

[11] Barsalou (1986, in press), a psychologist, has offered evidence that our judgments of prototypicality are not as stable as Rosch's initial data suggested. Barsalou takes this as indicating that concepts might not be fixed units stored in long-term memory, but temporary structures constructed on the fly from deeper units, a view that is compatible with Lakoff's view of concepts and category judgments.

relationship between cognitive science and neuroscience would look different when viewed as involving the development of an interfield theory than when construed as a case of theory reduction. In particular, I tried to show how the relationship would emerge as part of the endeavor of developing mechanistic explanations and showed some of the strategies involved in developing such mechanistic explanations. I have also tried to show how the framework of interfield theories provides a perspective for exploring relationships between disciplines in cognitive science, something for which the Theory Reduction Model was not designed.

Like many of the attempts in recent philosophy of science to provide alternatives to the Positivists' account (see chapter 4), the account of interfield theories is not nearly so precise as the Theory Reduction Model. In part this is due to the fact that it is not grounded primarily on principles of logic, but on empirical investigations of actual attempts to bridge disciplinary boundaries. Darden and Maull developed their account from a set of examples of interfield research they had analyzed and openly acknowledged that the account would require modifications as new cases were examined. The illustrations of cross-disciplinary endeavors presented in the last two sections of this chapter represent further empirical exploration of the character of cross-disciplinary endeavors. Because the emerging account is based on actual cases, it lacks the a priori prescriptive character of the Theory Reduction Model. The endeavors within cognitive science are material upon which to build the model, and not simply to be judged on the basis of the model. This is not to say, however, that the account of cross-disciplinary relationships will be altogether devoid of normative character. Insofar as it is based on analyses of both successes and failures of the past, it can provide guidance as to what strategies for integrating disciplines are likely to be successful. Moreover, if it is based on correct challenges to the Theory Reduction Model, it can serve the useful function of helping to dispel mythical accounts of how disciplines relate which, if not dispelled, may do much to hamper the development of valuable cross-disciplinary pursuits.

Postscript

In this volume I have presented a variety of views that philosophers of science have advanced concerning the character of scientific investigations in general and relations between disciplines in science in particular. As should be evident from the variety of views discussed, philosophy of science is not a discipline that has reached settled conclusions about the issues discussed. Rather, it is a discipline in transition. The views of the Logical Positivists, which dominated philosophy of science earlier in this century, have been largely rejected, but no successor has achieved the status Positivism once enjoyed.

Even in its unsettled state, however, philosophy of science can be useful to cognitive science. It offers a variety of perspectives from which we can examine the investigations being pursued in cognitive science in an attempt to understand these investigations. These perspectives can be useful to cognitive scientists as they try to chart future paths for their investigations. However, a caution is also in order. The perspectives offered by philosophy of science lack apodictic certainty. They are rather fallible attempts to use tools of human inquiry to understand how we conduct such inquiry. Although I encourage other cognitive scientists to take up the issues traditionally addressed by philosophers and to consider the views advanced by philosophers, you must maintain a critical perspective. This volume has attempted to provide you with a sufficient introduction into the issues of philosophy of science and the views advanced that you can enter the discussion. Once you engage the issues, however, you must also assume responsibility for the views you adopt, defending them for yourself. Do not take philosophers as final authorities!

References

Abrahamsen, A. A. (1987). Bridging boundaries versus breaking boundaries: Psycholinguistics in perspective. *Synthese, 72,* 355-388.

Abrahamsen, A. A. (in preparation). *Bridging interdisciplinary boundaries: The case of kin terms.*

Anderson, A. R., & Belnap, N. D., Jr. (1975). *Entailment* (Vol. 1). Princeton: Princeton University Press.

Armstrong, S. L., Gleitman, L., & Gleitman, H. (1983). What some concepts might not be. *Cognition, 13,* 263-308.

Ayer, A. J. (1963). *Logical positivism.* New York: The Free Press.

Bacon, F. (1620). *Novum organon.* London: J. Billium.

Barnes, B. (1977). *Interests and the growth of knowledge.* London: Routledge & Kegan Paul.

Barsalou. L. (1986). The instability of graded structures: Implications for the nature of concepts. In U. Neisser (Ed.), *Concepts and conceptual develpment: Ecological and intellectual factors in categorization* (pp. 101-140). Cambridge, England: Cambridge University Press.

Barsalou, L. (in press). Intra-concept similarity and its implications for inter-concept similarity. In S. Vosniadou & A. Ortony (Eds.), *Similarity and analogy.* Cambridge, England: Cambridge University Press.

Barsalou, L. W., & Sewall, D. R. (1984) Constructing representations of categories from different points of view. In *Emory Cognition Report #2.* Atlanta, GA: Emory University.

Barwise, J. (1987). Unburdening the language of thought. *Mind and Language, 2,* 82-96.

Barwise, J., & Perry, J. (1983). *Situations and attitudes.* Cambridge, MA: MIT Press.

Bechtel, W. (1982). Two common errors in explaining biological and psychological phenomena. *Philosophy of Science, 49,* 549-574.

Bechtel, W. (1984). Reconceptions and interfield connections: The discovery of the link between vitamins and coenzymes. *Philosophy of Science, 51,* 265-292.

Bechtel, W. (1985a). Realism, instrumentalism, and the intentional stance. *Cognitive Science, 9,* 473-497.

Bechtel, W. (1985b). Teleological functional analyses and the hierarchical organization of nature. In N. Rescher (Ed.), *Teleology and natural science* (pp. 26-48). Landham, MD: University Press of America.

Bechtel, W. (1986a). The nature of scientific integration. In W. Bechtel (Ed.), *Integrating scientific disciplines* (pp. 3-52). Dordrecht: Martinus Nijhoff.

Bechtel, W. (1986b). Building interlevel pathways: The discovery of the Embden-Myerhof pathway and the phosphate cycle. In J. Dorn & P. Weingartner (Eds.), *Foundations of biology* (pp. 65-97). Vienna: Holder-Pichler-Tempsky.

Bechtel, W. (1986c). What happens to accounts of the mind-brain if we forego an architecture of rules and representations? In A. Fine & P. Machamer (Eds.), *PSA 1986* (Vol. 1, pp. 159-171). East Lansing, MI: Philosophy of Science Association.

Bechtel, W. (in press a). *Philophy of mind: An overview for cognitive science.* Hillsdale, NJ: Lawrence Erlbaum Associates.

Bechtel. W. (in press b). Perspectives on mental models. *Behaviorism, 17.*

Bechtel, W., & Richardson, R. C. (in preparation). *A model of theory development: Localization as a strategy in scientific research.*

Berlin, B., & Kay, P. (1969). *Basic color terms: Their universality and evolution.* Berkeley: University of California Press.

Bloor, D. (1976). *Knowledge and social imagery.* London: Routledge & Kegan Paul.

Bloor, D. (1981). The strength of the strong program. *Philosophy of the Social Sciences, 11,* 199-213.

Blumenthal, A. L. (1987). The emergence of psycholinguistics. *Synthese, 72,* 313-324.

Boring, E. G. (1930). A new ambiguous figure. *American Journal of Psychology, 42,* 444-445.

Boveri, T. (1903). Über die Konstitution der chromatischen Kernsubstanz. *Verhandlungen der duetschen zoologischen gesellschaft zu Würzburg, 13,* 10-13.

Bradie, M. (1986). Assessing evolutionary epistemology. *Biology and Philosophy, 1,* 401-459.

Bradley, D., Garrett, M., & Zurif, E. (1980). Syntactic defects in Broca's aphasia. In D. Caplan (Ed.), *Biological studies of mental processess* (pp. 269-286). Cambridge, MA: MIT Press.

Bridgman, P. W. (1927). *The logic of modern physics.* New York: Macmillan.

Broca, P. (1861). Remarques sur le siege de la faculte du langage articule, suivies d'une observation d'aphemie. *Bulletin de la Societe Anatomique de Paris, 6,* 343-357.

Brodmann, K. (1909). *Vergleichende localisationslehre der grosshirninde in ihren prinzipien dorgestellt ouf grund des zellenbaues.* Leipzig: Barth.

Bromberger, S. (1968). An approach to explanation. In R. J. Butler (Ed.), *Analytic philosophy: Second series* (pp. 72-105). Oxford: Blackwell.

Brooks, L. (1978). Nonanalytic concept formation and memory for instances. In E. Rosch & B. B. Lloyd (Eds.), *Cognition and categorization* (pp. 169-211). Hilsldale, NJ: Lawrence Erlbaum Associates.

Brown, H. (1979). *Perception, theory, and commitment: The new philosophy of science.* Chicago: The University of Chicago Press.

Campbell, D. T. (1969). Ethnocentrism of disciplines and the fish-scale model of omniscience. In M. Sherif & C. W. Sherif (Eds.), *Interdisciplinary relations in the social sciences* (pp. 328-348). Chicago: Aldine.

Campbell, D. T. (1974a). Evolutionary epistemology. In P. A. Schilpp (Ed.), *The philosophy of Karl Popper* (Vol. 1, pp. 413-463). LaSalle, IL: Open Court.

Campbell, D. T. (1974b). 'Downward causation' in hierarchically organized biological systems. In F. Ayala & T. Dobzhansky (Eds.), *Studies in the philosophy of biology* (pp. 179-186). Berkeley: University of California Press.

Carnap, R. (1923). Über die Aufgabe der Physik und die Andwendung des Grundsatze der Einfachstheit. *Kant-Studien, 28,* 90-107.

Carnap, R. (1936). Testability and meaning. *Philosophy of Science, 3,* 420-468.

Carnap, R. (1937). Testability and meaning. *Philosophy of Science, 4,* 1-40.

Carnap, R. (1938). Logical foundations of the unity of science. In O. Neurath, R. Carnap, & C. Morris (Eds.), *International encyclopedia of unified science* (Vol. 1, pp. 42-62). The University of Chicago Press.

Carnap, R. (1956). The methodological character of theoretical concepts. In H. Feigl & M. Scriven (Eds.), *Minnesota studies in the philosophy of science* (Vol. 1, pp. 33-76). Minneapolis: University of Minnesota Press.

Carnap, R. (1967). *The logical structure of the world* (R. A. George, Trans.). Berkeley: University of California Press. (Originally published, 1928)

Causey, R. L. (1977). *Unity of science.* Dordrecht: Reidel.

Causey, R. L. (1984). Review of Mario Bunge, *The mind-body problem: A psychobiological approach. Synthese, 60,* 459–466.

Chisholm, R. M. (1976). *Theory of knowledge* (2nd ed.). Englewood Cliffs, NJ: Prentice-Hall.

Chisholm, R. M. (1982). *The foundations of knowing.* Minneapolis: The University of Minnesota Press.

Chisholm, R. M., & Schwartz, R. J. (1973). *Empirical knowledge: Readings from contemporary sources.* Englewood Cliffs, NJ: Prentice-Hall.

Chomsky, N. (1959). Review of Skinner's *Verbal behavior. Language, 35,* 26–58.

Chomsky, N. (1968). *Language and mind.* New York: Harcourt, Brace, & World.

Churchland, P. M. (1979). *Scientific realism and the plasticity of mind.* Cambridge, England: Cambridge University Press.

Churchland, P. M. (1984). *Matter and consciousness: A contemporary introduction to the philosophy of mind.* Cambridge, MA: MIT Press/Bradford Books.

Churchland, P. M., & Churchland, P. S. (1981). Functionalism, qualia, and intentionality. *Philosophical Topics, 12,* 121-145.

Churchland, P. M., & Hooker, C. A. (Eds.). (1985). *Images of science. Essays on realism and empiricism with a reply from Bas C. van Fraassen.* Chicago: University of Chicago Press.

Churchland, P. S. (1980). Language, thought, and information processing. *Nous, 14,* 147-170.

Churchland, P. S. (1986). *Neurophilosophy: Toward a unified science of the mind-brain.* Cambridge, MA: MIT Press/Bradford Books.

Clark, H. H., & Clark, E. V. (1977). *Psychology and language: An introduction to psycholinguistics.* New York: Harcourt, Brace, Jovanovich.

Crick, F. H. C. (1984). Function of the thalamic reticular complex: The searchlight hypothesis. *National Academy of Sciences of the United States of America. Proceedings. Biological Sciences, 81,* 4586-4590.

Darden, L. (1986). Relations amongst fields in the evolutionary synthesis. In W. Bechtel (Ed.), *Integrating scientific disciplines* (pp. 113-123). Dordrecht: Martinus Nijhoff.

Darden, L. (1987). Viewing the history of science as compiled hindsight. *AI Magazine, 8* (2), 33-41.

Darden, L., & Maull, N. (1977). Interfield theories. *Philosophy of Science, 43,* 44-64.

Darden, L., & Rada, R. (in press). Hypothesis formation using part-whole interrelations. In D. Helman (Ed.), *Analogical reasoning.* Dordrecht: Reidel.

Dennett, D. C. (1978). *Brainstorms.* Cambridge, MA: MIT Press/Bradford Books.

Dennett, D. C. (1981). True believers: The intentional strategy and why it works. In A. F. Heath (Ed.), *Scientific explanations* (pp. 53-75). Oxford: Clarendon Press.

Descartes, R. (1970). Meditations on first philosophy. In E. S. Haldan & G. R. T. Ross (Eds.), *The philosophical works of Descartes* (pp. 181-200). Cambridge, England: Cambridge University Press. (Originally published, 1641)

Duhem, P. (1954). *Aim and structure of physical theory.* New York: Antheneum. (Originally published, 1906)

Enc, B. (1983). In defense of the identity theory. *Journal of Philosophy, 80,* 279-298.

Feigl, H. (1970). The 'orthodox' view of theories: Remarks in defense as well as critique. In M. Radner & S. Winokur (Eds.), *Minnesota studies in the philosophy of science* (Vol. 4, pp. 3-16). Minneapolis: University of Minnesota Press.

Feyerabend, P. K. (1962). Explanation, reduction, and empiricism. In H. Feigl & G. Maxwell (Eds.), *Minnesota studies in the philosophy of science* (Vol. 3, pp. 28-97). Minneapolis: University of Minnesota Press.

Feyerabend, P. K. (1963a). How to be a good empiricist—A plea for tolerance in matters epistemological. In B. Baumrin (Ed.), *Philosophy of science. The Delaware seminar* (Vol. 2, pp. 3-40). New York: Interscience.

Feyerabend, P. K. (1963b). Materialism and the mind-body problem. *The Review of Metaphysics, 17,* 49-67.

Feyerabend, P. K. (1965). Problems of empiricism. In R. Colodny (Ed.), *Beyond the edge of certainty* (pp. 145-260). Englewood Cliffs, NJ: Prentice-Hall.

Feyerabend, P. K. (1970). Against method: Outline of an anarchistic theory of knowledge. In M. Radner & S. Winokur (Eds.), *Minnesota studies in the philosophy of science* (Vol. 4, pp. 17-130). Minneapolis: University of Minnesota Press.

Feyerabend, P. K. (1975). *Against method.* London: New Left Books.

Fitsch, G., & Hitzig, E. (1870). Ueber die elektrische Erregbarkeit des Grosshirns. *Archiv für Anatomie, Physiologie, und wissenschaftliche Medicin,* pp. 308-314.

Flourens, J. P. M. (1824). *Recherches experimentales sur les proprietes et les fonctions du systeme nerveux dans les animaux vertebres.* Paris: Crevot.

Fodor, J. A. (1974). Special sciences (Or: Disunity of science as a working hypothesis). *Synthese, 28,* 97-115.

Fodor, J. A. (1975). *The language of thought.* New York: Coswell.

Fodor, J. A. (1978). Propositional attitudes. *The Monist, 61,* 501-523.

Fodor, J. A. (1980). Methodological solipsism considered as a research methodology in cognitive psychology. *The Behavioral and Brain Sciences, 3,* 63-109.

Fodor, J. A. (1983). *The modularity of mind.* Cambridge, MA; MIT Press/Bradford Books.

Fodor, J. A. (1987). A situated grandmother? Some remarks on proposals by Barwise and Perry. *Mind and Language, 2,* 65-81.

Gall, F. J. (1835). *Sur les fonctions due cerveau et sur celles de chacune de ses parties* (W. Lewis, Trans.). (Originally published, 1809)

Geschwind, N., & Kaplan, E. (1962). A human cerebral disconnection syndrome. *Neurology, 12,* 675-685.

Gettier, E. L. (1963). Is justified true belief knowledge? *Analysis, 25,* 121-123.

Gholson, B., & Barker, P. (1985). Kuhn, Lakatos, and Laudan: Applications in the history of physics and psycholoy. *American Psychologist, 40,* 755-769.

Gibson, J. (1979). *The ecological approach to perception.* Boston: Houghton Mifflin.

Giere, R. N. (1979). *Understanding scientific reasoning.* New York: Holt, Rinehart & Winston.

Gleitman, L. R., & Gleitman, H. (1970). *Phrase and paraphrase: Some innovative uses of language.* New York: Norton.

Glotzbach, P., & Heft, H. (1982). Ecological and phenomenological contributions to the phenomenology of perception. *Nous, 16,* 108-121.

Glymour, C. (1980). *Theory and evidence.* Princeton: Princeton University Press.

Goldman, A. (1986). *Epistemology and cognition.* Cambridge, MA: Harvard University Press.

Goodman, N. (1947). The problem of counterfactual conditionals. *Journal of Philosophy, 44,* 113-128.

Goodman, N. (1955). *Fact, fiction, and forecast.* Cambridge, MA: Harvard University Press.

Gregory, R. L. (1961). The brain as an engineering problem. In W. H. Thorpe & O. L. Zangwill (Eds.), *Current problems in animal behavior* (pp. 307-330). Cambridge, England: Cambridge University Press.

Gregory, R. L. (1968). Models and the localization of functions in the central nervous system. In C. R. Evans & A. D. J. Robertson (Eds.), *Key papers in cybernectics* (pp. 91-102). London: Butterworth.

Grice, H. P., & Strawson, P. F. (1956). In defense of a dogma. *Philosophical Review, 65,* 141-158.

Grodzinsky, Y., Swinney, D., & Zurif, E. (1985). Agrammatism: Structural deficits and antecedent processing disruptions. In M. L. Kean (Ed.), *Agrammatism* (pp. 65-81). New York: Academic Press.

Gutting, G. (1980). *Paradigms and revolutions.* South Bend: University of Notre Dame Press.

Hanson, N. R. (1958). *Patterns of discovery.* Cambridge, England: Cambridge University Press.

Hanson, N. R. (1960). Is there a logic of discovery? In H. Feigl & G. Maxwell (Eds.), *Current issues in the philosophy of science* (pp. 20-35). New York: Holt, Rinehart, & Winston.

Hanson, N. R. (1967). An anatomy of discovery. *The Journal of Philosophy, 64*, 321-352.

Hebb, D. O. (1949). *The organization of behavior.* New York: Wiley.

Heider [Rosch], E. (1971). 'Focal' color areas and the development of color names. *Developmental Psychology, 4*, 447-455.

Heider [Rosch], E. (1972). Universals in color naming and memory. *Journal of experimental psychology, 93*, 10-20.

Hempel, C. G. (1962). Deductive-nomological vs. statistical explanation. In H. Feigl & G. Maxwell (Eds.), *Minnesota studies in the philosophy of science* (Vol. 3, pp. 98–169). Minneapolis: University of Minnesota Press.

Hempel, C. G. (1965). Aspects of scientific explanation. In C. G. Hempel (Ed.), *Aspects of scientific explanation and other essays in the philosophy of science.* New York: Macmillan.

Hempel, C. G. (1966). *Philosophy of natural science.* Englewood Cliffs, NJ: Prentice-Hall.

Hempel, C. G. (1970). On the 'standard conception' of scientific theories. In M. Radner & S. Winokur (Eds.), *Minnesota studies in the philosophy of science* (Vol. 4, pp. 142-163). Minneapolis: University of Minnesota Press.

Hesse, M. (1980). *Revolutions and reconstructions in the philosophy of science.* Bloomington, IN: Indiana University Press.

Holland, J., Holyoak, K., Nisbett, R., & Thagard, P. (1986). *Induction: Processes of inference, learning, and discovery.* Cambridge, MA: MIT Press.

Hooker, C. A. (1981). Towards a general theory of reduction. *Dialogue, 20*, 38-59; 201-236; 496-529.

Hooker, C. A. (1987). *A realistic theory of science.* Albany, NY: State University Press of New York.

Horgan, T. (1987). Cognition is real. *Behaviorism, 15*, 13-25.

Hughes, G., & Cresswell, M. J. (1968). *Introduction to modal logic.* London; Methuen.

Hull, D. (1974). *The philosophy of biological science.* Englewood Cliffs, NJ: Prentice-Hall.

Hume, D. (1888). *A treatise of human nature.* Oxford: Clarendon Press. (Originally published, 1740)

Kahneman, D., Slovic, P., & Tversky, A. (1982). *Judgment under uncertainty: Heuristics and biases.* Cambridge, England: Cambridge University Press.

Kaplan, R. M., & Bresnan, J. (1982). Lexical-functional grammar: A formal system for grammatical representation. In J. Bresnan (Ed.), *The mental representation of grammatical relations* (pp. 173-281). Cambridge, MA: MIT Press.

Katz, J. J. (1964). Analyticity and contradiction in natural language. In J. A. Fodor & J. J. Katz (Eds.), *The structure of language: Readings in the Philosophy of language* (pp. 519-543). Englewood Cliffs, NJ: Prentice-Hall.

Kauffman, S. (1971). Articulation of parts explanations in biology and the rational search for them. In R. C. Bluck & R. S. Cohen (Eds.), *PSA 1970* (pp. 257-272). Dordrecht: Reidel.

Kay, P., & McDaniel, C. (1978). The linguistic significance of the meanings of basic color terms. *Language, 54*, 610-646.

Klima, E., & Bellugi, U. (1979). *The signs of language.* Cambridge, MA: Harvard University Press.

Knoor, K. D. (1981). *The manufacture of knowledge: Towards a constructivist and contextual theory of science.* Oxford: Pergamon.

Kuhn, T. S. (1970a). *The structure of scientific revolutions* (2nd ed.). Chicago: University of Chicago Press. (Originally published, 1962)

Kuhn, T. S. (1970b). Reflections on my critics. In I. Lakatos & A. Musgrave (Eds.), *Criticism and the growth of knowledge* (pp. 237-278). Cambridge, England: Cambridge University Press.

Kyburg, H. E. (1968). *Philosophy of science: A formal approach.* New York: Macmillan.

Lakatos, I. (1970). Falsification and the methodology of scientific research programmes. In I. Lakatos & A. Musgrave (Eds.), *Criticism and the growth of knowledge* (pp. 91-196). Cambridge, England: Cambridge University Press.

Lakatos, I. (1978). History of science and its rational reconstructions. In J. Warrall & G. Currie (Eds.), *The methodology of scientific research programmes. Philosophical papers of Imre Lakatos* (Vol. 1, pp. 102-138). Cambridge, England: Cambridge University Press.

Lakoff, G. (1987). *Women, fire, and dangerous things: What categories reveal about the mind.* Chicago: University of Chicago Press.

Lakoff, G., & Johnson, M. (1980). *Metaphors we live by.* Chicago: University of Chicago Press.

Langley, P., Simon, H. A., Bradshaw, G. L., & Zytkow, J. M. (1987). *Scientific discovery: Computational explorations of the creative process.* Cambridge, MA: MIT Press.

Latour, B., & Woolgar, S. (1979). *Laboratory life: The social construction of scientific facts.* Beverly Hills: Sage.

Laudan, L. (1977). *Progress and its problems.* Berkeley: University of California Press.

Laudan, L. (1981). The psuedo-science of science. *Philosophy of the Social Sciences, 11,* 173-198.

Laudan, L., Donovan, A., & Laudan, R. (in press). *Scrutinizing science: Empirical studies of scientific change.* Dordrecht: Reidel.

Laudan, L., Donovan, A., Laudan, R., Barker, P., Brown, H., Leplin, J., Thagard, P., & Wykstra, S. (1986). Scientific change: Philosophical models and historical research. *Synthese, 69,* 141-223.

Lehrer, K. (1974). *Knowledge.* Oxford: Oxford University Press.

Leplin, J. (1984). *Scientific realism.* Berkeley: University of California Press.

Levi, I. (1967). *Gambling with truth: An essay on induction and the aims of science.* Cambridge, MA: MIT Press.

Liebig, J. (1842). *Animal chemistry or organic chemistry in its application to physiology and pathology* (W. Gregory, Trans.). Cambridge, England: John Owen.

Lloyd, E. (1984). A semantic approach to the structure of population genetics. *Philosophy of Science, 51,* 242-264.

Lycan, W. G. (1981). Form, function, and feel. *The Journal of Philosophy, 78,* 24-49.

Machamer, P. (1977). Teleology and selection processes. In R. G. Colodny (Ed.), *Logic, laws, and life: Some philosophical complications* (pp. 129-142). Pittsburgh: University of Pittsburgh Press.

Mates, B. (1972). *Elementary logic.* New York: Oxford University Press.

Maull, N. (1977). Unifying science without reduction. *Studies in the History and Philosophy of Science, 8,* 143-162.

McCauley, R. N. (1981). Hypothetical identities and ontological economizing: Comments on Causey's program for the unity of science. *Philosophy of Science, 48,* 218-227.

McCauley, R. N. (1986a). Intertheoretic relations and the future of psychology. *Philosophy of Science, 53,* 179-199.

McCauley, R. N. (1986b). The role of theories in a theory of concepts. In U. Neisser (Eds.), *Concepts and conceptual development: Ecological and intellectual factors in categorization* (pp. 288-309). Cambridge, MA: Cambridge University Press.

McCauley, R. N. (1987a). The role of cognitive explanations in psychology. *Behaviorism,15,* 27-40.

McCauley, R. N. (1987b). The not so happy story of the marriage of linguistics and psychology, or why linguistics has discouraged psychology's recent advances. *Synthese, 72,* 341-354.

McCawley, J. D. (1981). *Everything that linguists have always wanted to know about logic.* Chicago: University of Chicago Press.

McClelland, J. L., Rumelhart, D. E., & the PDP Research Group. (1986). *Parallel distributed processing: Explorations in the microstructures of cognition. Vol. 2: Psychological and biological models.* Cambridge, MA: MIT Press/Bradford Books.

McCloskey, M. E. (1983). Intuitive physics. *Scientific American, 248*(4), 122-130.

McCloskey, M. E., & Glucksberg, S. (1978). Natural categories. Well-defined or fuzzy set? *Memory and Cognition, 6,* 462-472.

Medin, D. L., & Ortony, A. (in press). Psychological essentialism. In S. Vosniadou & A. Ortony (Eds.), *Similarity and anological reasoning.* New York: Cambridge University Press.

Medin, D. L., & Schaffer, M. M. (1978). Context theory of classification learning. *Psychological Review, 85,* 207-238.

Miller, G. A. (1962). Some psychological studies of grammar. *American Psychologist, 17,* 748-762.

Miller, G. A., Galanter, E., & Pribram, K. H. (1960). *Plans and the structure of behavior.* New York: Holt.

Miller, G. A., & Johnson-Laird, P. (1976). *Language and perception.* Cambridge, MA: Harvard University Press.

Minsky, M. & Papert, S. (1969). *Perceptrons.* Cambridge, MA: MIT Press.

Murphy, G. L., & Medin, D. L. (1985). The role of theories in conceptual coherence. *Psychological Review, 92,* 289-316.

Mynatt, C. R., Doherty, M. E., & Tweney, R. D. (1978). Consequences of confirmation and disconfirmation in a simulated research environment. *Quarterly Journal of Experimental Psychology, 30,* 395-406.

Nagel, E. (1961). *The structure of science.* New York: Harcourt, Brace.

Neisser, U. (1975). *Cognition and reality: Principles and implications of cognitive psychology.* San Francisco: Freeman.

Neisser, U. (1986). From direct perception to conceptual structure. In U. Neisser (Ed.), *Concepts and conceptual development: Ecological and intellectual factors in categorization.* Cambridge, MA: Cambridge University Press.

Neuberg, C., & Kerb, J. (1913). Über zucherfreie Hefegärungen. XII. Über die Vorgänge der Hefegärung. *Zeitschrift für physiologische Chemie, 70,* 326-350.

Neurath, O. (1932). Protokollsatze. *Erkenntnis,3,* 204-214.

Newell, A., Shaw, J. C., & Simon, H. A. (1962). The process of creative thinking. In H. E. Gruber, G. Terrell, & M. Werheimer (Eds.), *Contemporary approaches to creative thinking* (pp. 63-119). New York: Atherton.

Nickles, T. (1973). Two concepts of intertheoretic reduction. *The Journal of Philosophy, 70,* 181-210.

Nickles, T. (1978). Scientific problems and their constraints. In R. Asquith & I. Hacking (Eds.), *PSA 1978* (Vol. 1, pp. 134-148). East Lansing, MI: Philosophy of Science Association.

Nickles, T. (1980a). Can scientific constraints be violated rationally? In T. Nickles (Ed.), *Scientific discovery: Logic and rationality* (pp. 285-315). Dordrecht: Reidel.

Nickles, T. (1980b). *Scientific discovery: Case studies.* Dordrecht: Reidel.

Nickles, T. (1980c). Introductory Essay: Scientific discovery and the future of philosophy of science. In T. Nickles (Ed.), *Scientific discovery: Logic and rationality* (pp.1-59). Dordrecht: D. Reidel.

Nisbett, R., & Wilson, T. (1977). Telling more than we can know: Verbal reports on mental processes. *Psychological Review, 84,* 231-259.

O'Keefe, J., & Nadel, L. (1978). *The hippocampus as a cognitive map.* Oxford: Clarendon Press.

Olds, J. (1965). Pleasure centers in the brain. *Scientific American, 195,* 106-116.

Osherson, D., & Smith, E. E. (1981). On the adequacy of prototype theory as a theory of concepts. *Cognition, 9,* 35-58.

Palmer, S., & Kimchi, R. (1986). The information processing approach to cognition. In T. Knapp & L. Robertson (Eds.), *Approaches to cognition: Contrasts and controversies* (pp. 37-77). Hillsdale, NJ: Lawrence Erlbaum Associates.

Pellionisz, A., & Llinas, R. (1982). Space-time representation in the brain. The cerebellum as a predictive space-time metric tensor. *Neuroscience, 7,* 2249-2970.

Pellionisz, A., & Llinas, R. (1985). Cerebellar function and the adaptive feature of the central nervous system. In A. Berthoz & G. Melvill Jones (Eds.), *Adaptive mechanisms in gaze control* (pp. 223-232). Amsterdam: Elsevier.

Polanyi, M. (1958). *Personal knowledge.* Chicago: University of Chicago Press.

Popper, K. R. (1959). *The logic of discovery.* London: Hutchinson. (Originally published, 1935)

Popper, K. R. (1965). *Conjectures and refutations: The growth of scientific knowledge* (2nd ed.). New York: Harper & Row.

Popper, K. R. (1972). *Objective knowledge: An evolutionary approach.* Oxford: Clarendon Press.

Putnam, H. (1962). The analytic and the synthetic. In H. Feigl & G. Maxwell (Eds.), *Minnesota studies in the philosophy of science* (Vol. 3, pp. 350-397). Minneapolis: University of Minnesota Press.

Putnam, H. (1975a). Philosophy and our mental life. In H. Putnam (Ed.), *Mind, language, and reality: Philosophical papers of Hilary Putnam* (Vol. 2, pp. 291-303). Cambridge, MA: Cambridge University Press.

Putnam, H. (1975b). The meaning of 'meaning.' In H. Putnam (Ed.), *Mind, language, and reality: Philosophical papers of Hilary Putnam* (Vol. 2, pp. 215-271). Cambridge, MA: Cambridge University Press.

Putnam, H. (1978). *Meaning and the moral sciences.* London: Routledge & Kegan Paul.

Putnam, H. (1983). *Realism and reason.* Cambridge, England: Cambridge University Press.

Pylyshyn, Z. W. (1984). *Computation and cognition: Towards a foundation for cognitive science.* Cambridge, MA: MIT Press/Bradford Books.

Quine, W. V. O. (1961a). On what there is. In W. V. O. Quine (Ed.) *From a logical point of view* (2nd ed., pp 1-19). New York: Harper & Row. (Originally published 1953)

Quine, W. V. O. (1961b). Two dogmas of empiricism. In W. V. O. Quine (Ed.), *From a logical point of view* (2nd ed., pp. 20-46). New York: Harper & Row. (Originally published, 1953)

Quine, W. V. O. (1969a). Existence and quantification. In W. V. O. Quine (Ed.), *Ontological relativity and other essays* (pp. 91-113). New York: Columbia University Press.

Quine, W. V. O. (1969b). Epistemology naturalized. In W. V. O. Quine (Ed.), *Ontological relativity and other essays* (pp. 69-90). New York: Columbia University Press.

Quine, W. V. O. (1972). *Methods of logic.* New York: Holt, Rinehart & Winston.

Quine, W. V. O. (1973). *The roots of reference.* La Salle, IL: Open Court.

Quine, W. V. O. (1975). The nature of natural knowledge. In S. Guttenplan (Ed.), *Mind and language* (pp. 67-81). Oxford: Clarendon Press.

Quine, W. V. O., & Ullian, J. S. (1970). *The web of belief.* New York: Random House.

Reber, A. (1987). The rise and (surprisingly rapid) fall of psycholinguistics. *Synthese, 72,* 325-340.

Reese, H. W., & Overton, W. F. (1970). Models of development and theories of development. In L. R. Goulet & R. B. Baltes (Eds.), *Life-span development psychology* (pp. 115-145). New York: Academic Press.

Reichenbach, H. (1956). *Nomological statements and admissible operations.* Amsterdam: North Holland.

Reichenbach, H. (1966). *The rise of scientific philosophy.* Berkeley: University of California Press.

Rey, G. (1983). Concepts and stereotypes. *Cognition, 15,* 237-262.

Rey, G. (1985). Concepts and conceptions: A reply to Smith, Medin, and Rips. *Cognition, 19,* 297-303.

Richardson, R. C. (1979). Functionalism and reductionism. *Philosophy of Science, 46,* 533-558.

Richardson, R. C. (1980a). Intentional realism or intentional instrumentalism. *Cognition and Brain Theory, 3,* 125-135.

Richardson, R. C. (1980b). Reductionistic research programmes in psychology. In P. D. Asquith & R. N. Giere (Eds.), *PSA 1980* (pp. 171-183). East Lansing, MI: Philosophy of Science Association.

Richardson, R. C. (1986). Language, thought, and communication. In W. Bechtel (Ed.), *Integrating scientific disciplines* (pp. 263-283). Dordrecht: Martinus Nijhoff.

Rorty, R. (1965). Mind-body identity, privacy, and categories. *The Review of Metaphysics, 19,* 24-54.

Rosch, E. (1975). Cognitive representations of semantic categories. *Journal of Experimental Psychology: General, 104,* 192-233.

Rosch, E. (1978). Principles of categorization. In E. Rosch & B. B. Lloyd (Eds.), *Cognition and categorization* (pp. 28-48). Hillsdale, NJ: Lawrence Erlbaum Associates.

Rosch, E., & Mervis, C. (1975). Family resemblances: Studies in the internal structure of categories. *Cognitive Psychology, 7,* 573-605.

Rosenberg, A. (1985). *The structure of biological science.* Cambridge, England: Cambridge University Press.

Rosenblatt, F. (1962). *Principles of neurodynamics.* New York: Spartan.

Rumelhart, D. E., McClelland, J. L., & the PDP Research Group. (1986). *Parallel distributed processing. Explorations in the microstructures of cognition. Vol. 1: Foundations.* Cambridge, MA: MIT Press/Bradford Books.

Rumelhart, D. E. (1984). The emergence of cognitive phenomena from the sub-symbolic processes. *Proceedings of the sixth annual conference of the Cognitive Science Society* (pp. 59-62). Boulder, CO.

Ryle, G. (1949). *The concept of mind.* New York: Barnes & Noble.

Salmon, W. (1970). *Statistical explanation and statistical relevance.* Pittsburgh: University of Pittsburgh Press.

Salmon, W. (1984). *Scientific explanation and the causal structure of the world.* Princeton: Princeton University Press.

Schaffner, K. (1967). Approaches to reduction. *Philosophy of Science, 34,* 137-147.

Scheffler, I. (1967). *Science and subjectivity.* Indianapolis, IN: Bobbs Merrill.

Schnaitter, R. (1987). Behaviorism is not cognitive and cognitivism is not behavioral. *Behaviorism, 15,* 1-11.

Scriven, M. (1962). Explanations, predictions, and laws. In H. Feigl & G. Maxwell (Eds.), *Minnesota studies in the philosophy of science* (Vol. 3, pp. 170-230). Minneapolis: University of Minnesota Press.

Selfridge, O. G. (1955). Pattern recognition by modern computers. *Proceedings of the Western Joint Computer Conference.* Los Angeles, CA.

Sellars, W. (1963). *Science, perception, and reality.* London: Routledge & Kegan Paul.

Shapere, D. (1966). Meaning and scientific change. In R. Colodny (Ed.), *Mind and cosmos: Explorations in the philosophy of science* (pp. 41-85). Pittsburgh: University of Pittsburgh Press.

Shapere, D. (1984). *Reason and the search for knowledge.* Dordrecht: Reidel.

Simon, H. A. (1980). *The sciences of the artificial* (2nd ed.). Cambridge, MKA: MIT Press.

Skinner, B. F. (1957). *Verbal behavior.* New York: Appleton-Century-Crofts.

Smith, E. E., & Medin, D. L. (1981). *Categories and concepts.* Cambridge, MA: Harvard University Press.

Smith, E., Medin, D., & Rips, L. J. (1984). A psychological approach to concepts: Comments on Rey's "Concepts and Stereotypes." *Cognition, 17,* 265-274.

Smith, E. E., Shoben, E. J., & Rips, L. J. (1974). Structure and process in semantic memory: A featural model for semantic decisions. *Psychological Review, 81,* 214-241.

Smolensky, P. (in press). On the proper treatment of connectionism. *Behavioral and Brain Sciences, 11.*

Sober, E. (1984). *Conceptual issues in evolutionary biology.* Cambridge, MA: MIT Press.

Stalnaker, R. C. (1968). A theory of conditionals. In N. Rescher (Ed.), *Studies in logical theory. American Philosophical Quarterly Monograph Series* (pp. 98-112). Oxford: Basil Blackwell.

Sternberg, S. (1966). High-speed scanning in human memory. *Science, 153,* 652-654.

Suppe, F. (1977). The search for philosophical understanding of scientific theories. In F. Suppe (Ed.), *The structure of scientific theories* (pp. 3-241). Urbana: University of Illinois Press.

Suppes, P. (1968). The desirability of formalization in science. *Journal of Philosophy, 65,* 651-664.

Sutton, W. (1903). The chromosomes in heredity. *Biological Bulletin, 4,* 231-251.

Swinburne, R. G. (1971). The paradoxes of confirmation—a survey. *American Philosophical Quarterly, 8,* 318-330.

Taylor, R. (1978). *Introductory readings in metaphysics.* Englewood Cliffs, NJ: Prentice-Hall.

Thagard, P. (1980). Against evolutionary epistemology. In P. D. Asquith & R. N. Giere (Eds.), *PSA 1980* (pp. 187-196). East Lansing: Philosophy of Science Association.

Thagard, P. (in press). *Computational philosophy of science.* Cambridge, MA: MIT Press/Bradford Books.

Toulmin, S. (1972). *Human understanding: The collective use and evolution of concepts.* Princeton: Princeton University Press.

Tulving, E. (1983). *Elements of episodic memory.* Oxford: Clarendon Press.

Turing, A. M. (1950). Computing machinery and intelligence, *Mind, 59,* 433-460.

Tweney, R. D., Doherty, M. E., & Mynatt, C. R. (1981). *On scientific thinking.* New York: Columbia University Press.

Valenstein, E. S. (1973). *Brain control: A critical examination of brain stimulation and psychosurgery.* New York: Wiley.

Van Fraassen, B. C. (1980). *The scientific image.* Oxford: Clarendon Press.

Von Eckardt, B. (1978). Inferring functional localization from neurological evidence. In E. Walker (Ed.), *Explorations in the biology of language* (pp. 27-66). Cambridge, MA: MIT Press/Bradford Books.

Wason, P. C., & Johnson-Laird, P. N. (1972). *Psychology of reasoning: Structure and content.* Cambridge, MA: Harvard University Press.

Weimer, W. B., & Palermo, D. S. (1973). Paradigms and normal science in psychology. *Science Studies, 3,* 211-244.

Whitley, R. (1980). The context of scientific investigation, In K. D. Knorr, R. Krohn, & R. Whitley (Eds.), *The social process of scientific investigation* (pp. 297-321). Dordrecht: Reidel.

Whitley, R. (1982). The establishment and structure of the sciences as reputational organizations. In N. Elias, H. Martins, & R. Whitley (Eds.), *Scientific establishments and hierarchies. Sociology of the sciences* (Vol. 6, pp. 313-357). Dordrecht: Reidel.

Wierzbicka, A. (1987). *'Prototypes save': On the current uses and abuses of the concept 'prototype' in current linguistics, philosophy, and psychology.* Unpublished manuscript.

Wilkes, K. V. (1978). *Physicalism.* London: Routledge & Kegan Paul.

Wilkes, K. V. (1981). Functionalism, psychology, and philosophy of mind. *Philosophical Topics, 12,* 147-167.

Williams, M. B. (1970). Deducing the consequences of evolution: a mathematical model. *Journal of Theoretical Biology, 29,* 343-385.

Wimsatt, W. C. (1972). Teleology and the logical structure of function statements. *Studies in the History and Philosophy of Science, 3,* 1-80.

Wimsatt, W. C. (1976a). Reductionism, levels of organization, and the mind-body problem. In G. Globus, G. Maxwell, & I. Savodnik (Eds.), *Consciousness and the brain: A scientific and philosophical inquiry* (pp. 205-267). New York: Plenum Press.

Wimsatt, W. C. (1976b). Reductive explanation: A functional account, In R. S. Cohen, C. A. Hooker, A. C. Michalos, & J. van Evra (Eds.), *PSA-1974, Boston studies in the philosophy of science* (Vol. 32, pp. 671-710).

Wimsatt, W. C. (1979). Reduction and reductionism. In P. D. Asquith & H. Kyburg (Eds.), *Current research in philosophy of science* (pp. 352-377). East Lansing: Philosophy of Science Association.

Wimsatt, W. C. (1980). Reductionistic research strategies and their biases in the units of selection controversies. In T. Nickles (Ed.), *Scientific discovery: Case studies* (pp. 213-259). Dordrecht: Reidel.

Wittgenstein, L. (1953). *Philosophical investigations.* New York: Macmillan.

Woodhouse, M. (1984). *A preface to philosophy.* Belmont, CA: Wadsworth.

Wright, L. (1976). *Teleology explanations: An etiological analysis of goals and functions.* Berkeley: University of California Press.

Yngve, V. H. (1960). A model and an hypothesis for language structure. *Proceedings of the American Philosophical Society, 104,* 444-466.

Author Index

A

Abrahamsen, A. A., 72, 111, 112, 113, 114, 120
Anderson, A. R., 5, 120
Armstrong, S. L., 115, 120
Ayer, A. J., 29, 120

B

Bacon, F., 66, 120
Barker, P., 69, 70, 123, 125
Barnes, B., 65, 120
Barsalou, L., 30, 115, 117, 120
Barwise, J., 10, 120
Bechtel, W., 43, 57, 67, 78, 80, 88, 91, 92, 99, 100, 102, 103, 105, 106, 110, 120, 121
Bellugi, U., 113, 124
Belnap, N. D., 5, 120
Berlin, B., 114, 121
Bloor, D., 65, 121
Blumenthal, A. L., 11, 121
Boring, E. G., 46, 121
Boveri, T., 98, 121
Bradie, M., 14, 121
Bradley, D., 108, 121
Bradshaw, G. L., 67, 125
Bresnan, J., 113, 124

B

Bridgman, P. W., 21, 121
Broca, P., 103, 121
Brodmann, K., 103, 121
Bromberger, S., 39, 121
Brooks, L., 115, 121
Brown, H., 29, 49, 70, 121, 125

C

Campbell, D. T., 14, 36, 99, 111, 121
Carnap, R., 20, 22, 26, 72, 121, 122
Causey, R. L., 72, 74, 95, 122
Chisholm, R. M., 13, 122
Chomsky, N., 56, 112, 122
Churchland, P. M., 68, 79, 89, 91, 122
Churchland, P. S., 72, 75, 79, 83, 85, 86, 91, 96, 122
Clark, E. V., 113, 122
Clark, H. H., 113, 122
Cresswell, M. J., 5, 124
Crick, F. H. J., 87, 122

D

Darden, L., 67, 97, 98, 122
Dennett, D. C., 92, 105, 122
Descartes, R., 11, 122
Doherty, M. E., 37, 66, 126, 129
Donovan, A., 70, 125

Duhem, P., 42, *122*

Hume, D., 15, 26, *124*

E, F

Enc, B., 79, *122*
Feigl, H., 28, *122*
Feyerabend, P. K., 58, 59, 88, *122, 123*
Fitsch, G., 103, *123*
Flourens, J. P. M., 81, *123*
Fodor, J. A., 10, 76, 77, 81, 91, *123*

G

Galanter, E., 56, *126*
Gall, F. J., 81, *123*
Garrett, M., 108, *121*
Geschwind, N., 107, *123*
Gettier, E. L., 12, *123*
Gholson, B., 69, *123*
Gibson, J., 100, *123*
Giere, R. N., 49, *123*
Gleitman, H., 113, 115, *120, 123*
Gleitman, L., 113, 115, *120, 123*
Glotzbach, P., 100, *123*
Glucksberg, S., 31, *125*
Glymour, C., 49, *123*
Goldman, A., 13, *123*
Goodman, N., 25, 27, *123*
Gregory, R. L., 104, *123*
Grice, H. P., 44, *123*
Grodzinsky, Y., 108, *123*
Gutting, G., 57, *123*

H

Hanson, N. R., 44, 66, *123, 124*
Hebb, D. O., 61, *124*
Heft, H., 100, *123*
Heider [Rosch], E., 115, *124*
Hempel, C. G., 23, 24, 26, 28, *124*
Hesse, M., 65, *124*
Hitzig, E., 103, *123*
Holland, J., 67, *124*
Holyoak, K., 67, *124*
Hooker, C. A., 14, 68, 75, 85, 96, *122, 124*
Horgan, T., 91, *124*
Hughes, G., 5, *124*
Hull, D., 78, *124*

J

Johnson, M., 116, *125*
Johnson-Laird, P., 36, 115, *126, 129*

K

Kahneman, D., 66, *124*
Kaplan, E., 107, *123*
Kaplan, R. M., 113, *124*
Katz, J. J., 44, *124*
Kauffman, S., 81, *124*
Kay, P., 114, *121, 124*
Kerb, J., 106, *126*
Kimchi, R., 92, *126*
Klima, E., 113, *124*
Knoor, K. D., 65, *124*
Kuhn, T. S., 52, 68, *124*
Kyburg, H. E., 28, *124*

L

Lakatos, I., 60, 62, *124, 125*
Lakoff, G., 116, *125*
Langley, P., 67, *125*
Latour, B., 65, *125*
Laudan, L., 63, 65, 70, *125*
Laudan, R., 70, *125*
Lehrer, K., 13, *125*
Leplin, J., 68, 70, *125*
Levi, I., 49, *125*
Liebig, J., 80, *125*
Llinas, R., 87, *126*
Lloyd, E., 49, *125*
Lycan, W. G., 105, *125*

M

Machamer, P., 100, *125*
Mates, B., 8, *125*
Maull, N., 97, *122, 125*
McCauley, R. N., 84, 88, 91, 92, 97, 112, 117, *125*
McCawley, J. D., 7, *125*
McClelland, J. D., 87, 109, *125, 128*

McCloskey, M. E., 31, 90, *125*
McDaniel, C., 114, *124*
Medin, D. L., 31, 115, 116, *125, 126, 128*
Mervis, C., 31, 115, *127*
Miller, G. A., 56, 112, *125, 126*
Minsky, M., 61, *126*
Murphy, G. L., 116, *126*
Mynatt, C. R., 37, 66, *126, 129*

N

Nadel, L., 105, *126*
Nagel., E., 23, 28, 72, *126*
Neisser, U., 100, 116, *126*
Neuberg, C., 106, *126*
Neurath, O., 20, *126*
Newell, A., 66, *126*
Nickles, T., 67, 68, 84, *126*
Nisbett, R., 67, 89, *124, 126*

O

O'Keefe, J., 105, *126*
Olds, J., 104, *126*
Ortony, A., 116, *125*
Osherson, D., 115, *126*
Overton, W. F., 69, *127*

P

Palermo, D. S., 69, *129*
Palmer, S., 92, *126*
Papert, S., 61, *126*
Pellionisz, A., 87, *126*
Perry, J., 10, *120*
Polanyi, M., 2, *126*
Popper, K. R., 14, 32, 34, 35, *126*
Probram, K. H., 56, *126*
Putnam, H., 44, 77, 79, 91, 115, *127*
Pylyshyn, Z. W., 96, *127*

Q, R

Quine, W. V. O., 8, 9, 14, 42, 43, 50, *127*
Rada, R., 67, *122*
Reber, A., 112, *127*
Reese, H. W., 69, *127*

Reichenbach, H., 18, 26, *127*
Rey, G., 115, 116, *127*
Richardson, R. C., 79, 97, 102, 103, 108, *121, 127*
Rips, L. J., 115, 116, *128*
Rorty, R., 88, *127*
Rosch, E., 30, 31, 115, *124, 127*
Rosenberg, A., 28, 78, *127*
Rosenblatt, F., 61, *127*
Rumelhart, D. E., 87, 109, *125, 128*
Ryle, G., 21, *128*

S

Salmon, W., 38, *128*
Schaffer, M. M., 115, *125*
Schaffner, K., 72, 83, *128*
Scheffler, I., 47, 57, *128*
Schnaitter, R., 57, *128*
Schwartz, R. J., 13, *122*
Scriven, M., 23, 39, *128*
Selfridge, O. G., 45, *128*
Sellars, W., 89, *128*
Sewall, D. R., 30, *120*
Shapere, D., 47, 57, 68, *128*
Shaw, J. C., 66, *126*
Shoben, E. J., 115, *128*
Simon, H. A., 66, 67, 102, *125, 126, 128*
Skinner, B. F., 55, *128*
Slovic, P., 66, *124*
Smith, E. E., 31, 115, 116, *126, 128*
Smolensky, P., 8, *128*
Sober, E., 10, *128*
Stalnaker, R. C., 26, *128*
Sternberg, S., 36, *128*
Strawson, P. F., 44, *123*
Suppe, F., 29, 49, *128*
Suppes, P., 28, *128*
Sutton, W., 98, *128*
Swinburne, R. G., 27, *128*
Swinney, D., 108, *123*

T

Taylor, R., 8, *128*
Thagard, P., 14, 67, 70, *124, 125, 128*
Toulmin, S., 14, 36, *128*
Tulving, E., 40, *128*

Turing, A. M., 21, *129*
Tversky, A., 66, *124*
Tweney, R. D., 37, 66, *126*, *129*

U, V

Ullian, J. S., 50, *127*
Valenstein, E. S., 104, *129*
Van Fraasen, 49, *129*
Von Eckardt, B., 107, *129*

W

Wason, P. C., 36, *129*
Weimer, W. B., 69, *129*
Whitley, R., 65, *129*

Wierzbicka, A., 116, *129*
Wilkes, K. V., 108, *129*
Williams, M. B., 28, *129*
Wilson, T., 89, *126*
Wimsatt, W. C., 67, 72, 77, 83, 84, 85, 100, *129*
Wittgenstein, L., 9, 30, 114, *129*
Woodhouse, M., 3, *129*
Woolgar, S., 65, *125*
Wright, L., 100, *129*
Wykstra, S., 70, *125*

Y, Z

Yngve, V. H., 114, *129*
Zurif, E., 108, *121*, *123*
Zytkow, J. M., 67, *125*

Subject Index

A

Aesthetics, 15
Analytic philosophy, 16, 43, 44
Analytic statements, 21, 41
  Analytic-synthetic distinction, 41–44, 56
Anomalies, 55
Autonomy of higher level disciplines,
  78–82, 92, 93, 107

B, C

Behaviorism, 2, 29–31, 55–57, 69, 75, 102,
  111
Categorization and concepts, 30–31,
  114–117
  prototype theories, 31, 115–117
Cognitivism, 2, 30, 57, 62, 69, 102
Confirmation and justification, 12–14,
  18–19, 32–37, 57, 60, 66, 75
Connectionism (parallel distributed process-
  ing theories), 56, 61, 109
Counterfactual claims, 26
Counterinduction (Feyerabend), 59
Covering law model, see Explanation,
  deductive-nomological model
Cross-Disciplinary Research, see also Theory
  Reduction, 87, 99, 101–118
  boundary-breaking, 111, 112
  boundary-bridging, 111, 114

research clusters, 71, 110, 111

D, E

Discovery, scientific, see also Theory reduction, co-evolution of theories 18, 60,
  65–68, 98–98, 102–107
  heuristics, role in 62, 66, 67
Ecological psychology, 100
Empiricists, see Logical Positivism
Epistemology, 3, 11–16, 43
  coherentist theories, 12, 13
  evolutionary epistemology, 14
  foundationalist theories, 12, 13
  naturalized epistemology, 14, 43
Ethics, 15
Existentialism, 16
Explanation, 22–29, 37–41, 71–75, 97–99,
  101–110
  causal, 38
  deductive-nomological model, 19, 22–27,
  29, 38–41, 71–75
  homuncular functionalism, 104–105
  inductive-statistical, 24
  mechanistic, 99, 101–110
  probabilistic, 24, 38

F

Falsificationism (Popper), 32–37

Folk psychology, 87–92
Functional analysis, 104–107

H, I

Hypothetico-deductive method, 22, 24–27, 30, 32
  Raven Paradox, 26
Incommensurability of Theories (Kuhn), 55–57, 88
Induction, 32–35, 66
Interfield theories, 97–101, 106–108, 110–118

J

Justification, *see* Confirmation

L

Laws, scientific, 19, 22–30, 37–41, 52, 58, 72–79, 94–97
  probabilistic laws, 24
Levels of organization, 72, 87, 100
Localizationist Research Programs 103–106, 109
Logic, 3–9, 18–20, 22–27, 33, 43, 66
  meta-theorems, 7
  modal logic, 26
  quantificational or predicate logic, 4, 6–9
  sentential or propositional logic, 4–7
  truth tables, 4, 5
Logical Positivism, 17–49, 50, 71–73
  theses of, 17–31
  criticisms of, 32–49

M

Meaning, verificationist theory of, 19–22, 26, 42–43
Metaphysics, 8–11, 19
  ontology, 8–11
    role in evaluating research programs, 63
    and Theory Reduction, 75, 96
Methodological anarchism (Feyerabend), 58

N, O

Normal science (Kuhn), 52–58, 61, 62
observation, 19–22, 30, 44–49, 55
  observation sentences, 20, 44
  theory-ladenness, 44–49, 55
Operational definitions, 21, 42, 43

P

Paradigm (Kuhn), 52–58
  exemplars, 53
Phenomenology, 16
Progress, scientific, 35, 51, 54, 55, 59–65, 69
Propositional attitudes, *see also* Folk psychology, 78

Q

Quine-Duhem thesis, 42

R

Reduction, *see* Theory reduction
Reduction sentences, 22
Research programmes (Lakatos), 60–63, 69
Research traditions (Laudan), 63–65, 69

S

Scientific revolutions (Kuhn), 55–57
Skepticism, 11, 14
Synthetic statements, 21, 41

T

Theories, scientific
  axiomatization of, 27–29
  underdetermination, 50
Theory reduction, *see also* interfield theories, cross-disciplinary research, 29, 71–97
  arguments opposed, 76–78, 94–97
  boundary conditions, 74
  bridge laws, 73, 74, 76–78, 82, 83, 85
  co-evolution of theories, 82–87

eliminative reduction, 87–92
Turing Test, 21

U, V

Unity of science, *see* Theory reduction and
Cross-disciplinary research

Value Theory, 14, 15
Verificationism, *see* Meaning, verificationist
theory of